T0339685

Cambridge Elements ≡

Elements in Ethics
edited by
Ben Eggleston
University of Kansas
Dale E. Miller
Old Dominion University, Virginia

DEONTOLOGY

Piers Rawling
Florida State University

CAMBRIDGE
UNIVERSITY PRESS

Shaftesbury Road, Cambridge CB2 8EA, United Kingdom

One Liberty Plaza, 20th Floor, New York, NY 10006, USA

477 Williamstown Road, Port Melbourne, VIC 3207, Australia

314–321, 3rd Floor, Plot 3, Splendor Forum, Jasola District Centre,
New Delhi – 110025, India

103 Penang Road, #05–06/07, Visioncrest Commercial, Singapore 238467

Cambridge University Press is part of Cambridge University Press & Assessment,
a department of the University of Cambridge.

We share the University's mission to contribute to society through the pursuit of
education, learning and research at the highest international levels of excellence.

www.cambridge.org
Information on this title: www.cambridge.org/9781108706520

DOI: 10.1017/9781108581196

First published 2023

A catalogue record for this publication is available from the British Library.

ISBN 978-1-108-70652-0 Paperback
ISSN 2516-4031 (online)
ISSN 2516-4023 (print)

Deontology

Elements in Ethics

DOI: 10.1017/9781108581196
First published online: January 2023

Piers Rawling
Florida State University

Author for correspondence: Piers Rawling, PRawling@admin.fsu.edu

Abstract: Deontology is a theory about how we should act, morally speaking. It comes in several varieties, but all share certain doctrines, many of which are close to those found in the so-called common-sense morality of the Western world. And all varieties are united in their opposition to consequentialism, a theory that, in its simplest form, tells us that we should always act so as to maximize impersonal value by bringing about the best consequences. This Element presents some of the different versions of deontology, including the views of W. D. Ross, and, to a lesser extent, Immanuel Kant. It defends certain deontological tenets, while challenging others, and contrasts them with consequentialism. Deontology and consequentialism are two of the main contenders in ethical theory, but virtue ethics is another, and it too is addressed (briefly), with an attempt to see it, in its most plausible form, as part of deontology.

Keywords: deontology, consequentialism, ethics, common-sense morality, duty

ISBNs: 9781108706520 (PB), 9781108581196 (OC)
ISSNs: 2516-4031 (online), 2516-4023 (print)

Contents

Introduction

'Deontology' is a term that is used in a variety of ways. Some definitions have it that deontology is an account of moral duty set out as a system of rules, as opposed to a theory (consequentialism) that assesses the morality of our actions in accord with the impersonal value of their consequences. Nagel (1986: 165, 175–80), on the other hand, gives an account of deontology in terms of reasons rather than rules. And according to him, if deontological reasons 'exist, they restrict what we may do in the service of either relative or neutral goals' (1986: 175), where neutral goals are associated with impersonal value, and relative goals with 'the desires, projects, commitments, and personal ties of the individual agent, all of which give him reasons to act in the pursuit of ends that are his own' (1986: 165).

Like both these accounts, I shall characterize deontology in part by its opposition to consequentialism. My focus in this regard will be the contrast between deontology and a simple form of consequentialism according to which we should always act so as to maximize value by bringing about the (impersonally) best consequences. Consequentialism comes in many varieties beyond this simple version (see Portmore, 2020), but I shall only address one other (rule consequentialism: see Section 4.6), and I shall not discuss attempts to 'consequentialize' all moral theories (see Dreier, 2011; Portmore, 2011). I should note that, while I am not a consequentialist, I do think that the flexibility of the view is sometimes underappreciated, and I shall frequently deploy consequentialist arguments against deontology – there being a distinction between deploying such arguments and arguing for full-blown consequentialism.

As regards particular deontologists, W. D. Ross and Immanuel Kant both more or less fit the bill, despite major differences in their theories. They are united (anachronistically) in their opposition to consequentialism, and both advocate moral rules, albeit of different kinds. I shall discuss both, but Kant to a far lesser extent (his ethics is the subject of Moran, 2022).

Contractualism (see Scanlon, 1998), which has Kantian elements, is a further ethical theory that might be considered a form of deontology (see McNaughton and Rawling, 2006, for discussion; it is also the subject of Suikkanen, 2020). As in Kantian ethics, and in contrast to Ross's view, contractualism's moral principles (such as a directive not to kill) derive from more basic considerations. Given that Kantianism has a clearer claim to being deontological, however, I shall use it as a contrast to Ross's position.

Deontology and consequentialism are two of the main contenders in normative ethical theory, but virtue ethics is another (the subject of Snow, 2020). Virtue ethics is addressed briefly right at the end of this Element (in Section 6.2), with an attempt to see it, in its most plausible form, as a part of deontology.

1 What Is Deontology?

1.1 Deontology and Consequentialism

In this section, I contrast deontology with the simple version of consequentialism mentioned in the previous section, according to which there is exactly one basic and overriding moral principle: we should act, on each and every occasion, so as to maximize the amount of good in the world – to bring about the best state of affairs that we can. (Unless otherwise noted, I shall use the term 'consequentialism' to refer to this simple version.) For the consequentialist, then, unlike the deontologist, the good determines the right. And different (simple) consequentialist theories are generated by differing accounts of what is good – utilitarianism (strictly speaking 'direct act hedonistic utilitarianism'), for example, famously holds that the one and only good is pleasure, and that we should maximize it with each act.

Here is an example sometimes used to contrast deontology with consequentialism. Imagine that you are in a position to quell an angry mob, and thereby save many innocent people, by killing an innocent person yourself. The consequentialist might argue that the good of the innocents saved would outweigh the bad of the one innocent killed, whereas the deontologist might well decry the appalling injustice of killing an innocent person, and contend that you should not kill them, regardless of the consequences.

As a result of this sort of example, some people see deontology as focused upon acts, and consequentialism as focused upon their consequences, where these are seen as distinct from the acts that give rise to them. But this is not the way that the distinction has been drawn more recently. According to Parfit, for example, consequentialism 'gives us one substantive moral aim: that history go as well as possible' (1984: 37), where history includes present, past, and future acts, as well as their consequences in the more ordinary sense.

Deontologists, on the other hand, claim that, even if making the world a better place (i.e., making history go better) is one moral goal (some might not accept even this), it is not the only one: the right is not determined by the good. (But note that its denial of consequentialism is only a necessary feature of deontology; other theories also deny it.) For example, some deontologists claim that there is an *absolute constraint* against intentionally killing an innocent person: doing so is always morally prohibited, even if it would produce more good – even if, indeed, intentionally taking the life of an innocent person yourself is the only way for you to prevent many more innocent people having their lives intentionally taken by other agents. The consequentialist, on the other hand, would contend that intentionally killing innocent people is bad, and thus the performance of such acts should, other things being equal, be minimized (in order to maximize the good by minimizing the bad) – so you may be morally required to kill an innocent person intentionally yourself if that is the only way to minimize such acts by others.

Other deontologists advocate for merely *threshold* constraints, where a threshold constraint is a proscription against certain kinds of acts, but only up to a certain threshold. Advocates of merely threshold constraints might maintain that, while killing the innocent is ordinarily forbidden, in a tragic case in which your killing an innocent person is the only way to prevent a calamity in which thousands of innocents would die, you may be permitted, or even required, to do it. This still contrasts with consequentialism, since on the latter view the threshold may be set considerably lower: the consequentialist might advocate that you are required to kill an innocent person yourself if that is the only way to save considerably fewer than thousands.

Deontology, then, not only denies that we are always required to maximize the good, it may require us not to, as in the case of the requirement not to violate a constraint even if you could maximize the good thereby. *Duties of special obligation* (sometimes referred to as duties of special relationship, directional duties, or positional duties) are another case in point: deontologists typically contend, for example, that you may be morally required to stick by your loved ones, even at significant personal cost, and even if you could maximize the good by abandoning them. Whereas the requirement not to violate constraints forbids us to harm *anyone* in the proscribed way, duties of special obligation are restricted: they apply only to our treatment of those to whom we bear the relationship in question, such as that of friendship, or promiser to promisee.

In contrast to these requirements not to maximize the good, in other cases deontology may merely give us permission – the *option* – not to do so. Deontology can be demanding, but on most versions many non-moral pursuits are permissible, innocent fun being one possibility. It is this that leaves room for *supererogation*. Supererogatory acts 'go beyond the call of duty': they are morally permitted and morally admirable (they typically involve self-sacrifice), but not morally required. Deontology may permit you to laze around next weekend, so that you are not required to spend it doing good deeds. Doing so would be supererogatory.

Consequentialism, on the other hand, leaves no room for supererogation: you are morally required to maximize the good, and you can do no more than this – it is impossible to go beyond the call of duty. This relentless requirement to maximize the good with every act also leads to the charge that consequentialism is both over-demanding and pervasive. For example, although the consequentialist may admit that innocent pleasure is a good, there is then the issue of how, as it were, to fit it in – your having fun is only allowed on the unlikely possibility that it maximizes the good (and then it is required, which perhaps rather spoils it).

1.2 Morality and Practical Reason

Practical reasons are reasons to do things (in contrast to theoretical reasons, which are reasons to believe things). And one question that arises about morality is its relationship to such reasons.

On one picture, consistent with that painted in the previous section, morality is seen as a system according to which acts fall into exactly one of three categories: the morally required, the morally permissible but not required, and the morally forbidden.[1] Practical reasons need not be part of this system. The question of what reason we have to do morality's bidding arises, rather, from outside the system. This view of morality is implicit in the following passage from Singer (Jamieson, 1999: 308–9):

> [Nagel and I] were discussing 'Famine, affluence and morality' [Singer, 1972], and Nagel was unable to accept that morality could be so demanding. But eventually it emerged that he was assuming that if morality did demand that we give so much to famine relief, then there must be overriding reason to do so. I was making no such assumption. On my view, I could recognize that if I were totally committed to doing what I ought to do, I would give away my wealth up to the point indicated in my article; but at the same time I may, without any irrationality, choose to be less than totally committed to doing what I ought to do. My own interests, or those of my family, may counteract the demands of morality to some degree, and I may think it reasonable to give in to them, while recognizing that it is morally wrong for me to do so. Once Nagel and I realized that we held these distinct understandings of morality, the practical difference between Nagel and myself over the demandingness of morality became less acute.

On Singer's view (at least as reflected in this passage; he has since changed his mind), then, morality and practical reasons are, to some extent at least, in different camps.

On an alternative view, moral reasons are a variety of practical reason, and a deontologist who appeals to them (on what I'll call the 'deontological reasons approach') might also countenance non-moral reasons. Even though there may be no sharp divide between the two, examples can be provided that are clearly on one side or the other. My reason to choose a peach over an apple – that the former is sweeter – is non-moral. My reason to give to Oxfam, on the other

---

[1] For the consequentialist, setting aside cases in which two or more acts are tied for being optimal, the second category is empty.

hand – that doing so will reduce innocent suffering – is moral. Or suppose that you promised to repay a debt on Thursday; this fact is a moral reason to do so. What about your reasons to favour your friends and family? Some object to the idea that any of these are moral on the grounds that there is something less than ideal about doing things for friends and family out of a sense of obligation. But, on one account, that is to confuse the issue of reason (in the sense here under consideration) with that of motivation: it's quite possible to do what your moral reasons favour – to rescue your child, say – out of affection.

On this deontological reasons approach, then, we each have a variety of practical reasons, some moral, some not. But do moral reasons always trump non-moral ones? I think not. Imagine you must break a relatively trivial promise if you are to pursue a great career opportunity. Surely you should break the promise (and apologize later). Even though you have most moral reason to keep the promise, this is outweighed by a reason of self-interest to pursue the career opportunity.

But is keeping the promise nonetheless morally required? If what you are morally required to do is what you have most moral reason to do, regardless of whether it is what you have most reason to do overall, then yes. However, it is now unclear what would count as a supererogatory act.

Alternatively, if an agent is morally required to perform some act just in case she has most reason overall to perform it where her 'winning' reasons are moral, then keeping the promise is not morally required. Is it supererogatory? This depends on how trivial the promise, and how great the career opportunity. The more trivial the former, and the better the latter, the more it looks as if it would be stupid rather than supererogatory to keep the promise. So, on this approach, it seems (roughly) that, in acting supererogatorily, you act on comparatively strong moral reasons, even though you do not do what you have most reason to.

This means, of course, that a supererogatory act is contrary to practical reason, in the sense that you have more reason to do something else. And this may run counter to intuition. However, it is a consequence of going beyond thinking of morality as merely a system of requirements, according to which a supererogatory act is morally admirable and permitted, but not morally required, no mention of reasons being necessary.

How does a reasons-based account of matters sit with consequentialism? If the consequentialist were to separate morality from practical reason, as in the passage from Singer earlier in this section, then, of course, the consequentialist could countenance all sorts of practical reasons, but the moral requirement to maximize the good would remain, and a key question would be whether you have most (or any) reason to do this.

Alternatively, the consequentialist could begin with the thought that what an agent has most reason to do is maximize the good. Consequentialism could still countenance practical reasons with a variety of contents, but, since it ranks acts in accord with the value of performing them, the combined net strength of an agent's reasons to perform an act would be proportionate to the amount of good she would do by performing it. That is, although the content of practical reasons need not reference the good on this consequentialist approach, reason strength would correlate with value, and value alone. And in performing the act for which she has the strongest reasons, the agent would be maximizing the good, and supererogation would be ruled out.

As regards contrasting the other components of deontology with consequentialism on a reasons-based account, constraints correspond to what I'll call 'constraining reasons'. Whereas the consequentialist advocates the maximization of value, the deontologist who claims that there are constraining reasons thinks there can be cases in which, for example, although it would maximize value for you to kill an innocent stranger, you have a stronger (constraining) moral reason not to. On this way of putting things, the advocate of an absolute constraint against killing innocents claims that the strength of your reason not to kill them is always infinite, whereas the advocate of a threshold constraint against such killing contends that there are finite constraining reasons: although the strength of your reason not to kill is finite, it can exceed the reason strength corresponding to the value of your not killing.

Duties of special obligation and options are captured in similar vein: you can have more moral reasons to favour those to whom you bear special relationships, or to engage in non-moral pursuits, than the value of your doing so would warrant.

On this approach, then, deontology is characterized, in part, by denying that reason strength is correlated only with value (see also Section 1.6) – you might have most reason, even most moral reason, to do something that is worse (in value terms) than some alternative.

1.3 Common-Sense Morality

Normative ethical theories can be classified as either accommodating or revisionary. Accommodating theories attempt to render ethical verdicts that accord with our 'common-sense' pre-theoretic moral judgements. Deontology can be seen as more accommodating in this sense than consequentialism – constraints, duties of special obligation, and the possibility of supererogation are all claimed to be components of 'common-sense morality', as is the idea that morality leaves room for non-moral pursuits.

Some consequentialists are radical reformers, and they argue for the overthrow of our common moral intuitions. But others might see these intuitions as playing an evidentiary role. Given this, one issue worth exploring is the extent to which the consequentialist can accommodate them. And, furthermore, for supporters of common-sense morality, it would be useful to know to what extent the consequentialist is forced to diverge from their common-sense views.

The consequentialist can argue that her theory is flexible, and that it can at least mimic much of common-sense morality – people may only believe in constraints, for instance, because they haven't considered unusual cases, and, in ordinary cases, violating constraints fails to maximize the good. In addition, the consequentialist can contend, in revisionary mode, that the deontologist's refusal to violate a constraint herself in order to prevent similar, but more numerous, violations by others can only be explained by a self-serving preference to keep her own hands 'clean'.

For instance, consider again the case in which you face the decision of whether to kill an innocent person to quell a riot, in order to save many other innocents. Some deontologists would prohibit such killing, invoking a constraint, whereas some consequentialists would advocate that you do it, in order to maximize the number of innocents saved. But they need not. Rather, the consequentialist could agree that it would be very bad, and, indeed, wrong. The difference with deontology, on this more sophisticated consequentialist account of the matter, would be evident in far-fetched circumstances in which your killing an innocent person to quell a riot is the only way in which to prevent many other people doing the same (killing innocents to quell riots). A deontologist who sees killing innocents to quell riots as a constraint violation would tell you not to kill here, whereas the consequentialist who thinks that killing innocents to quell riots is bad would tell you to minimize it, even if that requires doing it yourself – keeping your own hands clean will result in much more of the behaviour that you abhor. In ordinary circumstances, the practical upshot of the two proposals is, of course, the same: don't kill innocents to quell riots. But distinct prescriptions can result, as we have just seen, in far-fetched situations. This consequentialist strategy (dubbed 'the consequentialist vacuum cleaner' by myself and my frequent collaborator, David McNaughton) will recur often.

1.4 Consequences and States of Affairs

Some philosophers see deontology as differentiated from consequentialism in part by the latter's appeal to the states of affairs that agents bring about through their choices:

> In contrast to consequentialist theories, deontological theories judge the morality of choices by criteria different from the states of affairs those choices bring about. (Alexander and Moore, 2016: 3)

But this need not be. Both theories can be seen as concerned with the states of affairs we bring about through our actions. If there is an absolute constraint against intentionally killing innocent people, then you are prohibited from doing this – that is, you are prohibited from bringing about a state of affairs in which you intentionally kill an innocent person. And the consequentialist, her label notwithstanding, can, as we saw above, include an act within the state of affairs it brings about – indeed, the value of an act can be affected by events in the past. Consequentialists might, for instance, view the breaking of a promise, in itself, as bad, regardless of the future effects of doing so – a past commitment and its current violation can both contribute to the badness of a state in which this violation occurs. States of affairs can be viewed as histories, temporally extended into both the past and the future. Consequentialism can then be seen as imposing the moral requirement that we bring about the best temporally extended state of affairs that we can.

It is a mistake, on this broad account, to structurally assimilate all forms of consequentialism to one of its best-known forms, hedonistic utilitarianism, according to which pleasure is the only good, and we should maximize it. This view is only forward-looking: what you do today cannot influence the amount of happiness in the world yesterday. But consequentialism need not be seen as entailing that an act has a distinct temporal end point, with its consequences being confined to what it causes after this end point, and being in no way backward-looking.

Indeed, if consequentialism's notion of a consequence is narrowly construed in this latter way, consequentialism is placed under various unfortunate burdens. For example, if a consequence must be only forward-looking, then there is the danger of a puzzle arising when it comes to describing one and the same consequence in two different ways: one forward-looking and one backward-looking. Suppose a consequence of your mailing a letter is Fred's receiving a check. And suppose also that this event (Fred's receiving a check) constitutes repayment of your debt. The first description of this event is forward-looking, but the second description of that exact same event (your repaying Fred) is backward-looking. So is the event a consequence of your mailing the letter or not?

This puzzle does not arise on the broader construal of consequence, and this construal also enables the consequentialist to respond to two well-known deontological arguments against her position. Some deontologists argue that the distinction between doing and allowing is morally significant (see Section 2.2), as is that between the intended effects of our actions and their unintended but known side effects (see Section 2.1), but that the consequentialist cannot account for this. For example, whereas a deontologist might see euthanasia as wrong, since it is an intentional killing, she might view as permissible a doctor's allowing a terminally ill and suffering patient to die. And she might claim also that a doctor's administering a lethal dose of morphine to such a patient is permissible, provided that the doctor's intent is to alleviate suffering, even though the doctor knows that death will ensue as a 'side effect'.

On the narrow construal, consequentialism cannot draw these moral distinctions: the same narrow consequence, death, results in all three cases. So the 'narrow' consequentialist must argue either that these distinctions are not morally significant or that they cannot be adequately drawn. The 'broad' consequentialist, however, has a third way out, namely: she can point out that in doing versus allowing, or intended outcome versus unintended side effect, the histories are different, and thus, potentially, whatever the deontologist sees as accounting for the morally significant differences between the components within these two pairs, she can adopt as contributing differentially to the values of the relevant histories.

One response to either consequentialist approach, however, might be to challenge the very idea that states of affairs can bear value. Geach (1956: 41), for example, might be interpreted as claiming this:

> 'Event', like 'thing', is too empty a word to convey either a criterion of identity or a standard of goodness; to ask 'Is this a good or bad thing (to happen)?' is as useless as to ask 'Is this the same thing I saw yesterday?' or 'Is the same event still going on?', unless the emptiness of 'thing' or 'event' is filled up by a special context of utterance. Caesar's murder was a bad thing to happen to a living organism, a good fate for a man who wanted divine worship for himself, and ... a good or bad act on the part of his murderers; to ask whether it was a good or bad event would be senseless.

Geach makes his claim regarding events rather than states of affairs, but perhaps his complaint applies equally to the latter (assuming there is a difference): that dubbing a state of affairs 'good or bad would be senseless', because 'state of affairs' is 'too empty a word to convey ... a standard of goodness'. Geach may be correct that states of affairs are, strictly speaking, neither good nor bad simpliciter. But that does not preclude there being a scale of value with states of affairs being better or worse than one another: for instance, a state of affairs in which innocent people flourish is better than one in which they suffer.

Another response is to agree that states can be better or worse, but maintain that it is no part of our moral duty to produce better ones. Ethical egoism may be interpreted in this way. According to this theory, each of us has exactly one 'duty': to maximize our own well-being (or happiness). States of affairs can not only be ranked in terms of whether they are better or worse than one another simpliciter, but also in terms of whether they are better or worse *for individuals*. Ethical egoism is concerned only with the latter rankings, and urges each of us to promote states in which we do best for ourselves, regardless of whether this makes the world better or worse. Note that good for individuals has to be distinguished from good simpliciter, lest ethical egoism be incoherent. Moore failed to make this distinction in his (flawed) argument to the effect that ethical egoism is incoherent:

> What Egoism holds, therefore, is that *each* man's happiness is the sole good – that a number of different things are *each* of them the only good thing there is – an absolute contradiction! No more complete and thorough refutation of any theory could be desired. (1966 [1903]: 99)

(Moore did later recant this claim of incoherence (1912: 99–100).)

With the distinction between well-being and the good in place, however, ethical egoism can be seen as at least coherent, and the egoist can acknowledge that some states are better than others, but she does not see this as relevant to what she should do – all that is relevant for that is which state would benefit her the most.

Value and the good, as I shall use these terms, are, then, impersonal – or, more strictly (since, strictly speaking, it makes no sense to declare a state good or bad), states can be impersonally better or worse than one another. This is in contrast to one state being better *for someone or something* than another. Both measures are objective, but they measure different things. My unqualified use of 'good', 'value', 'better', and 'worse' will refer to the impersonal measures.

In line with their embrace of options, deontologists typically acknowledge that you have some reason to pursue your own well-being, but that is a far cry from the ethical egoist's claim that this is the only thing you have reason to pursue. And most deontologists also acknowledge both that states of the world can be better or worse, and that it is our moral duty to make the world a better place. But they deny the consequentialist claim that this is the only duty. As we shall see, for example, Ross thinks that we have a duty to 'produce as much good as possible' (1930: 27). But this is not our only duty; it has to be weighed against others (see Section 3.1).

1.5 Kant and Ross

So far I have focused upon deontology as contrasted with consequentialism. But deontology can also be characterized independently. Immanuel Kant and W. D. Ross may be seen as doing this.

The defining feature of Kantian ethics is the claim that moral prescriptions are generated from the *categorical imperative* (CI), the first, or universal law, formulation of which reads: 'Act only according to that maxim whereby you can at the same time will that it should become a universal law without contradiction' (Kant 1993 [1785]: 30). For Kant, if an agent behaves immorally, the maxim (or aim) on which she acts violates the CI, which is the moral law that a rational agent inevitably imposes on herself as a standard, on pain of contradiction, regardless of whether she always adheres to its dictates. The interpretation of Kant is notoriously controversial, but the CI can be seen as generating constraints and duties of special relationship, and admitting options. Thus Kant can be interpreted as a deontologist.

For example, suppose you act on the maxim of making promises that you have no intention of keeping (lying promises) whenever you stand to benefit from doing so. This is impermissible, according to the CI, because, if everyone did it, promising would be rendered impossible (no one would believe anyone's promises): you cannot will 'without contradiction' that everyone make lying promises whenever it is to their advantage, since everyone's doing this would, in the end, defeat its very possibility. A similar argument might be mounted against lying simpliciter: if everyone acted on the aim of deceiving whenever it was to their advantage, then communication would be disrupted to such an extent that the very possibility of lying would be undercut. Hence lying is impermissible: there is a constraint against it.

The duties not to lie and not to tell lying promises are what Kant terms 'perfect' duties: you are required to fulfil them perfectly by never lying and never telling a lying promise.

The duty to help others, by contrast, is an 'imperfect' duty: you are required to be helpful on occasion, but not on every occasion. In other words, on at least some occasions, you are required to adopt the ends of some others, in the sense of working to help them achieve some of their (permissible) aims. But which others, which of their aims, and when you choose to help are at your discretion. And this leaves room for options: provided we adhere to the perfect duties, and do something by way of fulfilling our imperfect duties, we are morally permitted to pursue other activities (at least on some interpretations of Kant).

Whereas failing to fulfil a perfect duty results in a contradiction in 'conception', according to Kant, failing to fulfil an imperfect duty gives rise to a contradiction 'in the will'.

A maxim yields a contradiction in conception if a world in which everyone acts on it is inconceivable: a world of lying promisers is inconceivable since there could be no promising in such a world; a world of liars is inconceivable since there could be no communication, and hence no lying, in such a world.

A maxim yields a contradiction in the will, on the other hand, if a world in which everyone acted upon it, while conceivable, cannot be 'rationally willed'. In the case of the imperfect duty to help others, for instance, each of us has good reason to pursue certain goals, but we need help to achieve them. So, if everyone acted on the maxim never to help anyone, we would be thwarted in our rational pursuits. Thus we should not always act on this maxim. We should help others sometimes.

However, among the objections typically raised to the first formulation of the CI are, first, that it does not rule out all acts that we consider wrong. Consider child abuse. There is presumably a perfect duty not to engage in this, and so acting on the maxim to abuse children should lead to a contradiction in conception, but it does not: a world in which everyone aims to abuse children is, although abhorrent, conceivable. Second, in justifying why something is wrong, we would expect to see an account of what makes it wrong, yet even if child abuse somehow did involve a contradiction in conception, such contradiction is not what makes it morally wrong (and similarly for lying and lying promises). And, third, many permissible acts seem to run afoul of this version of the CI. To give a standard example, the CI renders it impermissible to act on the maxim to always open doors for others, since it is not possible for everyone to do this.

Kant does, however, propose other formulations of the CI, and the humanity formulation may seem the most intuitively plausible: we should never act in such a way that we treat humanity, whether in ourselves, or in others, as a means only but always as an end in itself. This formulation is sometimes summed up as the requirement that we treat humanity with 'respect', which can be interpreted, in part, as forbidding us to treat people in ways to which they could not rationally consent (see Johnson and Cureton, 2021: 10–11). But, to return to the case of child abuse, the first difficulty is the extent to which children are capable of rational consent (a similar difficulty arises in the case of animal abuse), and, second, even if older children are rational in Kant's sense, and cannot rationally consent to abuse, this does not fully capture what makes it so wrong. But the humanity formulation does seem to fare better than the universal law formulation here. However, this raises the issue of the extent to which Kant's different formulations of the CI are equivalent. If the humanity formulation and the universal law formulation were to render different verdicts, this would show, of course, that they are not equivalent.

Some interpreters of Kant give prominence to the universal law formulation of the CI, others to the humanity formulation, and this results in two different interpretations of Kant (see Ebels-Duggan, 2011). Roughly speaking, those in the first group are Kantian 'constructivists': they see Kant as arguing that morality can be 'constructed' by means of 'formal' rational activity in conformity with the CI, with no substantive values or principles being presupposed. Those in the second group, on the other hand, might be dubbed Kantian 'realists': they see Kantian ethics as grounded in something of ultimate objective value (such as our humanity, interpreted, roughly, as our capacity to rationally choose and pursue goals). The constructivist interpretation provides the greater contrast to Ross (see Section 5), and, insofar as I presuppose either interpretation, it is this one.

Turning now to the good, the only things that are of *moral* worth, according to Kant, are good wills, acts motivated by a good will, and agents who have good wills, where an agent's will is good insofar as her actions are 'done not merely in conformity with duty (as a result of pleasant feelings) but from duty, which must be the true end of all moral cultivation' (2015 [1788]: 95).

There is, then, a key distinction for Kant between acting from desire or inclination and being moved to act by one's sense of duty. The morally good agent recognizes her duties, and does them from a sense of duty. And while inclination and duty might align, duty alone suffices in the morally good person. The virtuous agent takes it one step further. She is not merely someone who always acts from duty when required, but someone who also possesses strength of will, so that, should obstacles to her acting from duty arise, she would overcome them (someone might have the good fortune never to face such obstacles, and so manage to act from duty despite lacking such strength of will). (See Johnson and Cureton, 2021: 16–17.)

This notion of virtue features in Kant's account of the value (simpliciter) of a state of affairs, or possible world (as opposed to the moral worth of agents and their wills). The 'highest good', he claims, is the distribution of happiness to people in accord with their moral virtue:

> virtue and happiness together constitute possession of the highest good in a person, and happiness distributed in exact proportion to morality (as the worth of a person and his worthiness to be happy) constitutes the *highest good* of a possible world. (2015 [1788]: 90)

Next, according to Kant, 'we ought to strive to promote the highest good' (2015 [1788]: 101). Thus Kant can be seen (anachronistically) as agreeing with consequentialism that states of the world can be better or worse, and that we ought to promote the best one. But he does not see promoting the highest good as a duty distinct from those derived from the CI, rather, in doing as the CI prescribes, you are, roughly speaking, doing your part to promote the highest good. As Rohlf (2020: 23) puts it:

[T]he duty to promote the highest good is not a particular duty at all, but the sum of all our duties derived from the moral law [the CI] . . . [T]he duty of individuals is to promote (but not single-handedly produce) this end [the highest good] with all of their strength by doing what the moral law [the CI] commands.

The consequentialist might, of course, dispute whether the distribution of happiness in accord with virtue is the highest good, and will dispute the implicit claim that there are no possible circumstances in which violating a (supposed) constraint is necessary to most effectively promote it.

Kantian deontology also stands in contrast to other forms of deontology. I shall focus on that due to Ross (see Sections 3 and 4). One crucial point of contrast is that Kantian deontology is (purportedly) derived from one fundamental principle, the CI, whereas Ross (1988 [1930] ch. 2) claims that there are several distinct underivative moral considerations, which he formulates as a list of what he dubs 'prima facie duties'. These include duties of promise-keeping, gratitude, reparation, not harming others, and promoting the good. Another difference is that the duties Kant generates from the CI (supposedly) cannot conflict, whereas Ross's duties can. If, for example, keeping a promise will harm someone, then, on Ross's account, in order to determine what to do, the duty to keep the promise must be weighed against the duty not to harm, where this weighing is governed by no higher rule – it requires discernment and judgement.

1.6 Agent-relativity and Agent-neutrality

Another way to look at the difference between deontology and consequentialism is through the lens of the distinction between *agent-relative* and *agent-neutral* principles, reasons, or theories. Deontology is an agent-relative theory, whereas consequentialism is agent-neutral. (See Nagel, 1970, 1986; Parfit, 1984; McNaughton and Rawling, 1991.)

Here's a simple example to illustrate the distinction between agent-relative and agent-neutral principles. Suppose everyone is talking so loudly that no one can carry on a conversation. The advocate of a constraint against shouting will maintain that there is an agent-relative rule against doing so: nobody should shout, and, in particular, she shouldn't do so herself. Each person is primarily responsible for keeping her own voice in order. So she keeps her voice down. The advocate of an agent-neutral rule against shouting, on the other hand, thinks that the important thing is not that she, in particular, doesn't shout, but that the total amount of shouting is minimized. Each of us should try to get everyone to speak softly. So she shouts out: 'If everyone speaks softly, we'll all be able to hear one another.'

As we have seen, Kant notoriously claimed we should never lie – that there is an absolute constraint against lying. That is, each agent is responsible for ensuring that *she* doesn't lie, and this responsibility takes precedence over trying to instil honesty in others. Constraints are universal – they apply to everyone – but they are agent-relative in that each agent is primarily responsible for making sure that she toes the line, regardless of what others are doing. Deontology is an agent-relative theory, then, because it incorporates at least some agent-relative principles that take priority over what we might call their agent-neutral counterparts: a constraint against lying would be reflected in the claim that your duty not to lie yourself takes priority over your duty to try and ensure that nobody lies.

Duties of special obligation (assuming there are such) are also reflected in an agent-relative priority claim. For example, *I* owe a duty of care to *my* family, *you* to *yours*, and my duty to care for my own family takes priority over my trying to ensure that people in general care for their families.

Consequentialism can attempt to accommodate this duty by claiming that it's good to care for one's family, and thus familial caring is to be promoted. Typically, the best way to do this is for each of us to care for our own family. But suppose you can better promote familial caring overall by abandoning your own family to take a position in the government. The best way for you to follow the agent-neutral principle that tells each of us to ensure everyone cares for their own family would be to take the position. After all, your caring for your family is no more valuable than my caring for mine.

Similarly, the consequentialist might well see lying as bad (regardless of its effects), but, if so, this entails that, ceteris paribus, lying should be minimized: each of us should do our best to ensure that nobody lies. We won't be able to accomplish this goal, but at least we can try to minimize the bad behaviour. Typically, the best way for you to proceed is not to lie yourself, but what if you are in a situation in which you could set such a bad example with your lies that others are discouraged from pursuing the practice? Then the most effective thing you can do to promote honesty may be to lie yourself. The consequentialist claims, then, that the agent-relative directive not to lie yourself features merely as an instantiation of the agent-neutral directive to do your best to ensure that no one lies: you are just one of the people who shouldn't be lying. Each of us is directed to reduce the total amount of the bad conduct, regardless of whose conduct it is – your lying is no better or worse than anyone else's.

Consequentialism of the simple variety discussed here has, as we have seen, one fundamental principle: we should each do our best to maximize the good. But, on a pluralist account, the good has various components. And each of these components can be seen as corresponding to an agent-neutral principle derived from this fundamental principle. Lying is bad, so it gets its own derived agent-neutral prescription telling us, ceteris paribus, to minimize lying; and this takes precedence over your not lying yourself. Consequentialism is an agent-neutral theory because it contains no agent-relative principles that take precedence over their agent-neutral counterparts. But, on this sort of account, the derived agent-neutral principles are priority-ordered in accord with value: killing is worse than lying, so minimizing the former takes priority over minimizing the latter.

One complication is that some agent-relative rules and their agent-neutral counterparts are equivalent in their practical upshots. Consider again, for instance, the consequentialist requirement that each of us should maximize the good – that is, I should ensure that I do, and you should ensure that you do. Thus we have the appearance that consequentialism is agent-relative. But this directive is equivalent to its agent-neutral counterpart, which tells each of us to ensure that everyone does their part in maximizing the good: in order to achieve this goal, we have to coordinate and cooperate in the endeavour. The only way that I can maximize the good is to ensure that you and everybody else do too. Thus the agent-relative version of the rule does not take precedence over its agent-neutral counterpart, and consequentialism remains an agent-neutral theory.

There are other complications involved in precisifying this account of the agent-relative/agent-neutral distinction that I shall avoid here, but two points bear emphasizing.

First, both agent-relative and agent-neutral principles are universal. The agent-relative principle against lying tells all of us not to lie ourselves; the agent-relative principle concerning duties towards our families tells all of us to care for our own families. The agent-neutral counterparts of this pair tell all of us to minimize lying and promote familial caring, respectively.

Second, a theory's being agent-relative is not sufficient for it to be a version of deontology – for example, ethical egoism comprises one agent-relative rule: each of us should maximize our own well-being. And neither does a theory's being agent-neutral suffice for its being a form of consequentialism: a theory with one fundamental agent-neutral principle to the effect that each of us should ensure that everyone does their part in *minimizing* the good is agent-neutral.

So far, then, we have a distinction between agent-relative and agent-neutral principles, which yields a distinction between agent-relative and agent-neutral theories, where the latter distinction depends upon which principles take priority. But what about a distinction between agent-relative and agent-neutral reasons? Such a distinction is required, for example, if we want to characterize deontology on the reasons approach discussed in Section 1.2.

One attempt to distinguish agent-relative from agent-neutral reasons appeals to a difference in content, for example:

> An agent-relative reason is one that cannot be fully specified without pro-
> nominal back-reference to the person for whom it is a reason. .... An agent-
> neutral reason is one that can be fully specified without such an indexical
> device. (Pettit, 1987: 75)

But this account fails if the intent is to distinguish between deontology and consequentialism. For instance, when Andrew is asked why he is reading to some particular child, he might respond by saying, 'because she is *my* child'. Thus his reason appears to be agent-relative by this criterion. However, for all the content of his reason tells us, he could be a consequentialist who believes that the world goes best when parents read to their own children, and his reading to his child is the best he can do at present to promote this good behaviour. To emphasize the point, note that, if this is the case, the full specification of Andrew's reason still includes pronominal back-reference to himself: it's *his* reading to *his* child that is good here.

A more promising avenue is to look to what correlates with reason *strength*, as in Section 1.2. The idea, as applied to Andrew reading to his daughter, is that, if the strength of his reasons to read to her reflect only the amount of good his reading to her will do, then his reasons are all agent-neutral. If, on the other hand, this is not the case, then at least some of his reasons are agent-relative – if Andrew has a deontological duty of special obligation towards his daughter, for example, his reasons to read to her will have greater net strength than the value alone of his doing so would warrant.

Reasons for or against an action are made so by some consequence (which can be broadly construed to include the act itself and its history) that the action would likely bring about. That it's cold outside is a reason for you to put your coat on because it would keep you warm (the envisaged consequence). Keeping you warm is a good thing, but do you have more reason to keep warm than the value of your keeping warm warrants? (That is, does the reason strength generated by the benefit to you of your keeping warm exceed that generated by the contribution that this benefit makes to the overall good?) If no, then this reason of yours (that it's cold outside) to put your coat on is agent-neutral; if yes, then this reason is agent-relative – it has extra strength in addition to that dictated by the (impersonal) value of your keeping warm (although we might say it also has an agent-neutral component to account for the latter).

That your utterance would be a lie is a reason against uttering it because doing so would, let us suppose, harm someone's interests. If the strength of the reason you have not to make the utterance is proportionate to the badness of the harm it would cause, it is agent-neutral. If it is a stronger reason against your making the utterance than this, it is agent-relative. If the lie were going to be told to a stranger, this excess (negative) strength would reflect the presence of a constraint – or, rather, a constraining reason, as per Section 1.2 – against lying (and if the strength were infinite, the constraint would be absolute).

An agent's reason for or against performing some act is agent-neutral, then, if, and only if, its strength is proportionate to the value of its consequence relative to the reason in question. Thus, according to consequentialism, all our reasons are agent-neutral. But someone might posit that all we have reason to do is promote the bad, in which case, on his theory too, all reasons are agent-neutral. In the case of the lie mentioned earlier in this section, for example, on this view the fact that it would damage someone's interests counts in its favour, and its strength is proportionate to how bad this is. So again agent-neutrality is necessary, but not sufficient, as a criterion of consequentialism.

Agent-relative reasons (if such there be), on the other hand, are ones whose strength is not proportionate to value alone. And the deontologist claims that we have agent-relative reasons to do things, or not, on occasion (perhaps on many occasions). However, agent-relative reasons are not associated solely with deontology (the ethical egoist, for example, would contend that all our reasons are agent-relative). So the existence of agent-relative reasons is necessary but not sufficient for the truth of deontology.

It is important to note that reason strength here is an objective matter, in the sense that it is independent of how strong we may happen to think our reasons are, and also independent of desire strength: strong desires do not necessarily indicate strong reasons (we may have strong desires to do very foolish things – things we have overriding reasons not to do). But this objectivity merely requires a rank ordering: some reasons are stronger than others, just as, on the previous account, some principles take precedence over others.

2 Two Deontological Doctrines

Having introduced the basic elements of deontology, I turn now to a pair of doctrines that are commonly held by deontologists, and that might, if vindicated, be important in building a case against consequentialism. This section is largely independent of the others, and may be mostly skipped by readers who are less than enthralled by discussions of trolley problems and their ilk.

The first doctrine, that of double effect (DDE), focuses on the difference between what we intend[2] to do and what are mere side effects of our actions. The claim is that what is prohibited as an intended effect might be permitted as a side effect. The focus of the second doctrine, the doctrine of doing and

---

[2] It is possible to do something intentionally without having formed an intention to do it (I turn the steering wheel intentionally when driving, but I don't form an intention to do so each time I steer). So it may be possible to intentionally bring about an unintended side effect, but I shall endeavour to sidestep this potential complication in what follows.

allowing (DDA), is, as the name implies, the distinction between what we do and what we allow. Advocates of DDA claim that it is harder, morally speaking, to justify doing harm than to justify allowing it.

Although these doctrines are not entailed by the components of deontology so far discussed, they are associated with the view. For example, Nagel (1986: 179) says the following:

> I believe that the traditional principle of double effect, despite problems of application, provides a rough guide to the extension and character of deonto-logical constraints, and that even after the volumes that have been written on the subject in recent years, this remains the right point of convergence for efforts to capture our intuitions. The principle says that to violate deonto-logical constraints one must maltreat someone else intentionally. The mal-treatment must be something that one does or chooses, either as an end or as a means, rather than something one's actions merely cause or fail to prevent but that one doesn't aim at.

As regards DDA, Ross maintains that the duty of non-maleficence (not to harm others) is 'a duty distinct from that of beneficence [to better the condition of others], and [is] a duty of a more stringent character' (1930: 21), and he goes on to say that we 'should not in general consider it justifiable to kill one person in order to keep another alive' (1930: 22) (see also Sections 3.1 and 4.2). So on Ross's view inflicting harm (in violation of the duty of non-maleficence) is typically harder to justify than allowing it (in violation of the duty of beneficence).

Deontologists who argue for these doctrines, however, face several challenges. First it has to be established that there are robust differences between what we do by intent and what is a side effect, and between doing and allowing (I shall largely assume that there are). Then, assuming that these differences stand up to scrutiny, their moral significance has to be demonstrated. One challenge here comes from consequentialism (where by consequentialism, as previously, I mean the simple version according to which we should maximize the good with our every act). On a narrow construal of consequence, whether a given outcome of an act is intended or not, done or allowed, makes no difference to its consequences, and thus a consequentialist might deny that these distinctions make any difference to the value of an act, and thus no difference to its moral status. This comports with the commonly held supposition that DDE and DDA are non-consequentialist prin-ciples (see, e.g., Fitzpatrick, 2012; McIntyre, 2019; Nelkin and Rickless, 2014; Woollard and Howard-Snyder, 2021), and that establishing one or both of them would be a mark in favour of deontology, and against consequentialism.

But suppose that there are morally significant differences between what we do by intent and what is a side effect, and between doing and allowing. Then another consequentialist challenge arises: if consequence is construed broadly, consequentialism might well be able to accommodate the moral significance of these differences by valuing differently harm that is intended versus not, or done rather than allowed. The defender of deontology then has to defend specifically deontological versions of DDE and DDA.

A further challenge to these doctrines concerns their explanatory generality. The standard strategy for defending them begins by considering pairs of cases in which, despite the relative similarity of the scenarios depicted within the members of each pair, many of us have moral intuitions that render different verdicts about the moral permissibility of relatively similar courses of action within these scenarios. Advocates of DDE or DDA then argue that their favoured doctrine explains these intuitions. But their opponents claim either that the favoured doctrine fails to explain the correct verdicts in at least some of the cases to which it could be (or has been) applied, or that there is some other account of matters that is explanatory in more cases (including the ones to which the doctrine applies), or both.

Finally, there may be difficulties for DDE that become apparent when we consider an agent's reasons for pursuing one course of action (or inaction) rather than another.

I now turn to explore these doctrines and their challenges in more detail.

2.1 The Doctrine of Double Effect

Regarding constraints (see Sections 1.1 and 4.2), a distinction can be drawn between proscriptions against causing harm, and proscriptions only against inflicting intended harm. If constraints are seen as involving intent, then, while (typically) killing in the implementation of an intent to kill is forbidden, it may be that killing in the absence of such an intent is permissible in certain circumstances, such as when it will save many lives overall. The doctrine, or principle, of double effect (DDE) builds on this (putative) difference in permissibility.

Our actions have many effects, some of them intended, some not. In the standard simple cases used to illustrate DDE, two effects are considered (hence 'double effect'): an intended good effect, and an unintended harmful side effect that might render the act impermissible if intended. According to DDE, even if you know you will produce the harmful side effect, your action may nevertheless be morally permissible, provided that the good of the intended effect compensates for the harm of the unintended side effect, and you have done your best to minimize the harmfulness of this side effect. This is in contrast to cases in which you intend to inflict significant harm as a means of producing good, which is impermissible on views that impose constraints on such intended harming.

DDE is a traditional Catholic doctrine, and has its origins in Thomas Aquinas's (*Summa Theologica* (II-II, Qu. 64, Art. 7) 1988) argument for the permissibility of self-defence: killing your attacker may be permissible provided your intention is the preservation of your life, and not the killing of your attacker. (In addition, the killing must not be the result of a disproportionate use of force.)

DDE has many standard illustrations. Here are four.

The Trolley Problems

In one version of the well-known 'trolley problem' (Foot, 1967; Thomson, 1985), if you are to save five people from being killed by a runaway trolley, you must divert it onto another track by throwing a switch. But then it would kill one person on that track, and you know this. Call this 'trolley problem one'. Is throwing the switch morally permissible (or perhaps even morally required)? If you throw the switch, you would do so with the intention of saving the five, and killing the one would be an unintended side effect (or so some people argue). Thus, given that the good of five saved outweighs the one death, DDE might render the sacrifice at least permissible. Contrast this with a case (trolley problem two) in which you throw someone onto the track in order to stop the trolley and prevent it killing the five. Here (on one interpretation of matters) you intend to kill the one as a means to save the five (unlike the first case, you cannot accomplish your goal of saving the five without the presence of the one on the track). Hence DDE does not apply, and killing the one is impermissible on views that incorporate a constraint against intended killing of the innocent.

Transplant

Foot (1967) contrasts the possibility of a surgeon killing one person and then using his organs to save five others (I shall follow Thomson (1985) in calling this case 'Transplant') with that of denying one person a life-saving drug in order to distribute it to five others who each require only one-fifth the dose. In Transplant, the surgeon intends to kill the one, and so it is ruled out if there is a constraint against such killing. But in the drug case the death of the one might be seen as an unintended side effect, and hence permitted by DDE, due to the good of saving the five outweighing the bad of the one death.

Terror Bomber

The strategic bomber attacks military targets with the intention of destroying them, but tries to avoid civilian deaths – they are an unintended side effect ('collateral damage'). The terror bomber, on the other hand, intends to kill civilians in order to terrorize the enemy population, and so aims bombs at non-military targets. In the case of fighting a war against an evil aggressor, applying DDE may render strategic bombing, but not terror bombing, permissible, even if both varieties cause the same number of civilian casualties, and have a similar positive impact on defeating the enemy.

Palliative Care

If a terminally ill patient is in terrible pain, a doctor may be permitted, according to DDE, to administer palliative drug treatment with the intention of reducing the patient's suffering, even if she knows it will kill him, while she is forbidden to end the patient's suffering by administering exactly the same treatment if killing him is part of her intent. (It should be noted that this illustration is hypothetical. According to Fohr, for example: 'The belief that palliative care hastens death is counter to the experience of physicians with the most experience in this area. No studies have shown that patients' lives have been shortened through the administration of appropriate pain medication' (1998: 319). See also Sykes and Thorns, 2003.)

There is a vast literature on DDE, and its various challenges (see, e.g., FitzPatrick, 2012; McIntyre, 2019; Nelkin and Rickless, 2014). I shall now use the aforementioned cases as vehicles to discuss some of these.

One kind of challenge might focus on how robust a distinction there really is between intended effects of actions and their known side effects. In trolley problem one, for example, if you kill the one by diverting the trolley, it's not as though you did it by accident. But, in this case, perhaps, to say you did not kill the one by accident is merely to acknowledge that you knew it was going to happen – it was a *known* side effect. And the distinction between intended effects and known side effects is widely accepted in areas such as pharmaceutical medicine. The more common challenge, then, accepts the distinction between intended effects and known side effects, but raises questions about its moral significance, and how general an explanation DDE provides of the distinction between permissible and impermissible actions.

Consider, for example, Thomson's (1985: 1402) 'loop variant' of the trolley problem (call this 'trolley problem three'). In this version, when the track diverges, the trolley travels onto a track with (in contrast to the original version) a section added so that it circles back on itself. If the trolley goes left, it will travel in a clockwise direction, and hit and kill five people, whose bodies are, collectively, large enough to stop it before it goes on to kill a further person. If, on the other hand, it goes right, and proceeds in a counterclockwise direction, it will encounter this latter person first, and kill him, but his body is large enough by itself to stop the trolley, so the five others will be saved. The trolley is headed left, but you can throw a switch and divert it right to save the five. However, if you do so, it appears that you will intend to kill the one as a means to save the five, so DDE does not apply – as opposed to the situation in trolley problem one, in which the death of the one is an unintended side effect, and hence permitted by DDE. But, in Thomson's view, 'we cannot really suppose that the presence or absence of that extra bit of track makes a major moral difference as to what an agent may do in these cases' (1985: 1403). The cases are sufficiently similar that either you may divert in both cases or neither.

Let us suppose, then, that you may divert in both these cases. (This was Thomson's 1985 view, but she changed her mind in Thomson (2008) to the view that you may not divert in either case.) But this poses problems for DDE. First, DDE might predict a difference in permissibility between diverting in the loop variant (killing the one with intent) and throwing the switch in trolley problem one (killing the one as a known side effect). Second, DDE might explain the permissibility contrast between the first two trolley cases (permissibly throwing the switch versus impermissibly throwing someone on the track to stop the trolley), but it cannot explain the permissibility contrast between trolley problems two and three (both involve killing the one with intent). Furthermore, nor does it explain why it is permissible to divert in the loop variant but not permissible for the surgeon to operate in Transplant (again both involve killing the one with intent).

Thus there are difficulties for those who claim a wide explanatory role for DDE. Of course, if so, this merely shows that DDE's explanatory power is limited. However, it is preferable, of course, to have a unified way of explaining all the cases and their contrasts together, particularly if DDE fails explanatorily in further cases that supposedly illustrate it.

In the case of the terror bomber, for example, some argue that he does not actually intend the civilian deaths – rather, all he intends is to give the appearance of their deaths (see Nelkin and Rickless, 2014: 127–8). If he could give this same appearance without actually killing anyone, that's what he would do. If this is correct, then DDE fails to explain the contrast between terror and strategic bombing.

Nelkin and Rickless (2014) respond to this challenge by building on the work of Quinn (1989a) to propose a modified version of DDE:

> (DDE-R) In cases in which harm must come to some in order to achieve a good (and is the least costly of possible harms necessary), the agent foresees the harm, and all other things are equal, a stronger case is needed to justify harmful direct agency than to justify equally harmful indirect agency.
> (Nelkin and Rickless, 2014: 137)

Where harmful direct and indirect agency are defined (by Quinn) as follows:

> Harmful Direct Agency
> Agency in which harm comes to some victims, at least in part, from the agent's deliberately involving them in something in order to further his purpose precisely by way of their being so involved.

Harmful Indirect Agency

> Agency in which harm comes to some victims, but in which either nothing in that way is intended for the victims or what is so intended does not contribute to their harm. (Quinn, 1989a: 343)

There is some question as to whether DDE-R is a version of DDE, since intentions are not explicitly mentioned in the definition of harmful direct agency. But DDE-R is clearly in the spirit of DDE, with its implied reference to furthering a purpose by way of deliberately involving victims.

As regards terror bomber, even if he does not strictly intend the civilian deaths, it is hard to deny that he involves them in his plan 'to further his purpose precisely by way of their being so involved'. So, by the lights of DDE-R, terror bombing is harder to justify than strategic bombing, and this accords with most people's intuitions about the case.

How does DDE-R fare in other cases? In trolley problem one, killing the one would appear to be a case of harmful indirect agency, whereas killing the one in trolley problems two and three are cases of harmful direct agency. According to DDE-R, then, killing the one in trolley problem three (the loop variant) should be harder to justify than killing the one in trolley problem one. And perhaps it is (see Nelkin and Rickless, 2014, note 37, 154–5). But even if so, this need not render different verdicts concerning permissibility – it may be harder to justify killing the one in trolley problem three, but, nevertheless, the justification might go through in this case, but not in the case of trolley problem two (throwing someone on the track).

However, applying DDR-E to the palliative care case is even trickier. The idea would be, presumably, that administering the pain-relieving drug with the intention of killing the patient is harmful direct agency (we are assuming that the doctor harms the patient in killing him), whereas her killing him as a side effect would be harmful indirect agency. But in killing the patient with intent here, is the doctor 'deliberately involving [him] in something in order to further [her] purpose precisely by way of [his] being so involved'?

The difficulty can perhaps be brought out more clearly by looking to the rationale behind DDE-R. Again building on the views of Quinn (1989a), Nelkin and Rickless (2014) give a rights-based rationale for DDE-R derived from Kant's (1993 [1785]: 428–9) humanity formulation of the CI (see Section 1.5):

> We conclude that, on the strongest version of the Kantian rationale, the presumption against harmful direct agency derives from the fact that such agency infringes an independent right not to be made to serve others' purposes without one's consent. (Nelkin and Rickless, 2014: 133)

> While DDE-R specifies in detail at least one way of using another for one's purpose in such a way that harm comes to her, it is supported by a general moral

principle that appeals to the concept of a right. The fact that people have rights not to be treated in particular ways explains why harmful direct agency tends to be more difficult to justify than harmful indirect agency in certain circumstances. Their having rights is not part of the content of DDE-R; but their having rights explains why DDE-R is correct.

(Nelkin and Rickless, 2014: 151)

So the question is whether, in killing the patient with intent, the doctor is using him as a means only to serve her (the doctor's) purposes in relieving his (the patient's) suffering. This would seem to be a difficult case to make. Furthermore, as Thomson (1985: 1403) points out, this rationale does not seem to help us see why the killing of the one in the loop variant of the trolley problem is permissible (assuming it is), whereas the surgeon's killing the one in Transplant is not. The one in both cases would be used as a means only.

Insofar, then, as DDE-R and its rationale are proposed as having more general explanatory power than DDE, the jury would seem to be out. I turn now to the challenges from consequentialism.

The first is a simple frontal attack. On a narrow construal of consequence, the intention of the agent is no part of the consequence of her actions. On this construal, then, all that matters to the consequentialist in, say, the trolley cases or Transplant is the number of lives saved. And since killing the one saves the same net number (namely, four) in all of them, saving the five is permissible in all cases or none. And since death in these cases is bad, saving the five is not only permissible in all cases, but also required.

As noted previously, some consequentialists are radical reformers, and so they might argue against the common intuition that in, say, Transplant, the surgeon should not kill one random healthy person in order to save five other people by transplanting the one's organs into them. But the consequentialist who seeks to hew closer to common intuition can be more subtle about this latter case in various ways.

She might appeal to the bad effects of surgeons kidnapping people off the streets. No one would feel safe, and the psychological toll on the population, in combination with the killing of unwilling donors, might outweigh the good of saving the lives of the transplant recipients.

Or the consequentialist might take a broader view of consequence by evaluating possible histories of the world, and argue that a history in which surgeons intentionally sacrifice innocent people, even with the overall intent of saving lives, would be worse than a history in which the surgeons refrain and those lives are lost. This would be a consequentialist attempt to incorporate an ersatz version of DDE – there being two barriers to the consequentialist adoption of DDE proper, in its traditional form.

One is the fact that consequentialism is limited in its account of permissibility: any act that is permissible is required, unless two or more acts are tied in that they will produce the most good. So the consequentialist would have to say, in cases where producing the unintended side effect is permissible, that doing so is also required (in the absence of ties).

The other is the fact that consequentialism repudiates constraints, which, if they are formulated so as to involve intentions, DDE embraces. Thus the consequentialist cannot subsume the traditional version of DDE. But this may be grist to her mill, since, given her rejection of constraints, she also rejects this version of DDE: her standard complaint about constraints applies.

Consider Transplant again. Suppose a cabal of mad surgeons are busy kidnapping people off the street and harvesting their organs to save five times as many lives as they (the surgeons) sacrifice (and what they are doing is the only way to save these lives). The consequentialist and the deontologist can agree that this is a bad thing, and what the cabal is up to is morally wrong. Where the two disagree concerns what we should do about it.

We could come up with an imaginative scenario in which the only way to foil the mad surgeons is for some other surgeon, S, to harvest organs from some innocent victim, V, and use them to save five lives. The details do not matter, so long as in doing so S would intend to kill V in order to save the five lives, and would thereby prevent the other surgeons sacrificing many other potential victims (this being the only way for her to do so). The deontologist who favours a constraint against intended killing will declare that what S is proposing is morally wrong. The consequentialist will object on the usual grounds that if S doesn't act, then more of the bad acts that we are trying to prevent will be performed: S should proceed.

What about DDE-R? Rather than involving constraints, it appeals, as we have seen, to an underlying rationale involving our rights not to be used without our consent. As with constraints, consequentialism cannot accommodate rights. V has a right not be sacrificed without her consent, so the deontologist claims that S should respect this, and not proceed. The consequentialist, on the other hand, asks about the (purported) rights of all the other victims that would be violated if S were not to proceed – surely S should act so as to minimize the number of rights violations. On the consequentialist account, then, we have no rights in the deontologist's sense, since the deontologist denies that they can be 'traded off' in the manner proposed by the consequentialist. The deontological position is that, even if by violating someone's rights yourself you could minimize the number of such rights violations overall, you should not do it.[3] (See also Section 4.3.)

---

[3] At least, this is the case for absolute rights. The deontologist could (perhaps more plausibly) propose threshold rights in a manner analogous to threshold constraints.

So consequentialism can accommodate the badness of intended harmings by advocating that these be minimized, which might require that some intended harmings are perpetrated – something ruled out by deontology. And it can accommodate the badness of using some people as means to benefit others by advocating that such usings be minimized, which might require that some people be used – again, something ruled out by deontology. But the consequentialist might be accused at this point of arbitrarily adding intended harmings or usings to her list of those things considered bad. Why (as we are currently supposing the consequentialist claims) is intended harming worse than harming as a known side effect ('side effect harming')?

The consequentialist might respond by claiming that she can appeal to the same case that the deontologist makes for DDE. But the deontologist argues for a right or constraint against intended harming, both of which the consequentialist rejects. So does the deontologist have arguments for the right or constraint to which the consequentialist cannot appeal? We are back to the consequentialist's familiar arguments.

First, against those advocates of DDE (e.g., Nagel, 1986: 179) who appeal to moral intuitions, the consequentialist can press the question of whether our intuitions really support a right or constraint against intended harming that is not in place against side effect harming, as opposed to supporting the proposition that intended harming is worse than side effect harming.

And, second, in response to those advocates of DDE (or its close neighbours) who appeal to a rationale based on the idea that we have a right not be used by others in carrying out their plans, even to good ends (e.g., Quinn, and Nelkin and Rickless), the consequentialist can argue that the rationale merely supports the claim that being used is harmful.

Hence, if the deontologist can defend DDE, then the consequentialist who finds something in the vicinity of DDE compelling may be able to appeal to her own version of the deontologist's resources to accommodate an ersatz version of DDE and its underpinnings. And not only the consequentialist may do so, but also anyone who rejects constraints and rights, leaving the deontologist with the additional burden of defending these.

Finally, other potential concerns about DDE emerge when we consider reasons for action (practical reasons). Such reasons may be seen as falling into two categories: normative and motivating.

Normative reasons are facts: the fact that the ultraviolet (UV) index is high is a reason for you to apply sunblock. Note that there are two facts here. Fact one: the UV index is high. Fact two: fact one is a reason for you to apply sunblock. Fact two is a normative fact – a fact that embodies a normative element. Fact one, the reason, is not itself a normative fact in this case (although this is not always true), so the term 'normative reason' is something of a misnomer here, but it is now part of common philosophical parlance. (In the discussion of practical reason in Section 1.2, it is normative reasons that I have in mind.)

Motivating reasons, on the other hand, are (on one account) psychological states of the agent. If you applied sunblock, it might be that you did so because you *believed* the UV index was high, and that sunblock would prevent the UV radiation causing you sunburn,[4] and you *wanted* to avoid sunburn. If this is the case, then these psychological states explain why you did it. And, if you haven't done it yet, these psychological states (assuming you have them) comprise your motivation to apply your sunblock.

As regards motivating reasons, one apparent worry concerning DDE (raised, for instance, by Scanlon, 2008) is that you should be able to choose whether or not to do something that is morally impermissible, but that DDE removes this choice. Suppose that your performing some act, A, will save many people, but will harm someone, S. Suppose in addition that you take yourself to have good reason to harm S – you would benefit from it financially, say. So you have two motivating reasons to A: you believe that A-ing would save many people, and that it would benefit you financially. Suppose further that, in acting on only the first reason, you would intend to save the many but not to harm S, so that this is permissible according to DDE – indeed, let us suppose it is morally required. But if you were to act on the second reason (either by itself or in conjunction with the first), you would intend to harm S, which is impermissible by DDE's lights. Scanlon's claim (2008: 56–61) is that, if you were to A, you could not choose which reason you would be moved by, and hence, given DDE, you cannot choose to avoid doing something impermissible here: you must A, since A-ing with the intent only of saving the many is a moral requirement, but harming S with intent is impermissible, and you cannot choose with which intent you will A. This claim is subject to challenge, however. As Nelkin and Rickless put it (2014: 143): 'even if we cannot choose what to see as reasons, we do not see why we cannot choose to act on one rather than another'.

Let us turn now to normative reasons (in the following paragraphs I shall omit the 'normative'). In many cases, we don't deliberate about what to do, but when we do, roughly speaking we weigh up (what we take to be) our reasons for and against our various options, and (if acting rationally) choose to perform the act that we take to be favoured by the balance of our reasons. In trolley problem one (in its original form), for instance, your reason in favour of throwing the switch is that doing so would save five people; your reason against is that doing so would kill one person. In Transplant, similarly, the surgeon's reason in favour of

---

[4] If either of these beliefs is false, then, of course, you lack normative reason to apply sunblock.

operating is that she would save five lives; her reason against is that she would take one. Despite the similarities, some people's intuitions are that the reason in favour is the stronger in the trolley problem, but not in Transplant. As we have seen, according to DDE this disparity is due to a difference in intentions: the surgeon intends to kill the one in Transplant (if she intends the end of saving the five, she intends the means, which requires killing the one), whereas you don't intend to kill the one by throwing the switch in the trolley problem (killing the one is not a means to saving the five). However, as stated so far, this difference in intentions is not reflected in the practical reasons competing in the two cases.

If we are to follow DDE, then, we need to add the intentions of the agents to the picture. In Transplant, for instance, the fact that operating would require the surgeon to intend to kill the one might be considered a further reason against her doing so, or it might be considered a feature that strengthens that reason. In the trolley problem, the fact that, in throwing the switch, you would not intend to kill the one might be considered a reason in favour of throwing it, or a factor that weakens the force of the reason against throwing it.

Alternatively, the advocate of DDE might try introducing intentions into the acts rather than the reasons: that acting in a certain way would kill someone is a stronger reason against the act if it would involve killing with intent than if not.

However, problems ensue if we introduce intentions in any of these ways. Here's an illustration. Suppose, prior to adding intentions to the mix, you have reason to go out for a meal with friends (you would enjoy it), but this is marginally outweighed by your reason to visit a grumpy relative (you would not particularly enjoy it, but he would appreciate the visit, his grumpiness notwithstanding). But, if intentions weigh in the balance of reasons, then fun might well win out over duty: provided you can get yourself to form the intention to go out for the meal, then the fact that you so intend might add sufficiently to that side of the ledger to overcome the marginal weight advantage of your reason to visit your relative. Clearly something is awry. The fact that you intend to go out is not a normative reason to do so. Rather, rational agents typically form their intentions *based on* what they take themselves to have most reason to do (and, of course, *after* they have reached their view as to what this is).

There are exceptions to this, but they are what we might call perverse cases. Suppose a mind-reading evil demon has threatened calamity unless you form the intention to hurt your child – the demon cares not whether you actually do the deed, you just have to form the intention to do it (cf Kavka, 1983). So, assuming you can form it, your intention would not be based upon what you have most reason to do (you certainly do not have most reason to hurt your child). But note that, in this perverse case, the fact that you intend to hurt your child is a fortiori not a normative reason to do so.

If this claim that intentions are not reasons is correct, then, since DDE entails that intentions can contribute to moral wrongness, the advocate of DDE must deny that wrongness is only a matter of reasons. And perhaps this is not obviously incorrect, but it does open up possibilities that some may find counterintuitive. For example, suppose, in the palliative care case, that the doctor (correctly) thinks it for the best, and best for the patient, to administer a lethal dose of painkiller, and takes herself (correctly) to have most reason to do this, and thus forms the intention to do so. But now, as per DDE, she sees the fact that she intends to kill the patient as making it wrong to do so. Thus we have a case in which someone has most reason to do something that is morally forbidden – and, arguably, most *moral* reason to do this: it would be undertaken to alleviate pain and suffering.

And this example also brings out other difficulties. Given her predicament, the doctor has reason, if DDE holds, to set about modifying her intentions so that she intends only to relieve the patient's pain. But, at the least, trying to do this would waste her time and energy, even if she could succeed. More significantly, we can see from this case that DDE might give us reason to 'game' morality (see, e.g., Katz, 1996): if, say, the doctor, who seeks to do only what is morally permissible, stood to gain an inheritance from the patient's death, she would have even more reason to try and make it the case that his death would be an unintended side effect.

Finally, it should be noted that those who reject DDE need not deny that intentions play a moral role. It might be, for instance, that they count when it comes to the agent's blameworthiness. In Transplant, on this approach, the fact that the surgeon intends to kill would not contribute to the wrongness of doing so, but, if she were to operate, then the fact that she had intended to kill the victim might add to her blameworthiness for having done so.

So much for DDE. I turn now to the second doctrine commonly held by deontologists, that of doing and allowing.

2.2 The Doctrine of Doing and Allowing

According to the doctrine of doing and allowing (DDA), it is harder, morally speaking, to justify doing harm than to allow it, so that constraints might prohibit doing harm in cases where allowing a similar harm is permissible. As Foot (1967) notes, lest DDE and DDA be conflated, you can intend to allow something. And you can do things unintentionally. So intending does not always align with doing.

Recall trolley problem one: if you are to save five people from being killed by a runaway trolley, you must divert it onto another track by throwing a switch.

But then it would kill one person on that track, and you know this. Foot's (1967) original version of her trolley problem, however, is subtly different. You are driving the trolley. The brakes fail, and you are faced with the choice of steering it left or right. If you steer left, you will kill one person; if you steer right you will kill five. Contrast this case with Transplant (in which, recall, a surgeon is faced with either killing one or allowing five to die). Foot asks why the trolley driver should kill the one, while the surgeon should not. She acknowledges that DDE can provide an answer: the trolley driver does not intend to kill the one. But she also sees another possibility. She can be seen as invoking DDA (see Thomson, 1985): killing one is worse than letting five die (so the surgeon should not kill the one), but killing five is worse than killing one (so the trolley driver should steer left). And she prefers DDA because, in part, she sees it as covering more cases.

As regards the intuitive appeal of DDA, if we thought allowing people to die were on a par with killing them, we would, presumably, be far more devoted to averting humanitarian crises than we are. And active euthanasia would be no more controversial than passive. But does DDA withstand scrutiny?

Thomson (1985: 1397–9) introduces trolley problem one precisely to challenge Foot's claim that killing one is worse than letting five die, and thus challenge Foot's explanation of the intuition in Transplant that the surgeon should not kill the one. If you throw the switch in trolley problem one, you kill one; if you fail to throw the switch, you allow five to die. And, the thought is, it seems at best no worse to kill the one, and probably better to do so. And if killing one is not worse than letting five die in trolley problem one, we seem to have lost the DDA explanation of why the surgeon should not kill the one in Transplant (Thomson, 1985: 1399).

Another well-known problematic case for DDA is due to Rachels (1975). He contrasts situations in which two uncles stand to gain from the deaths of their nephews. In case one, the uncle drowns the child in the bathtub (thus doing harm); in case two, the uncle stands ready to do this, but the child drowns without his having to intervene (he thus allows harm). The circumstances are otherwise identical. Rachels sees no moral difference between the doing and allowing here, and concludes that, intrinsically, killing is no worse than letting die – when it is worse, that must be due to other factors.

One response to these cases is to claim that context makes a difference: just because there is no intrinsic moral difference between doing and allowing in one context, it does not follow that the same is true in all contexts. But now, as with DDE, DDA loses its purported explanatory generality.

Another response is to claim that we are not focusing on the right distinction. It is Thomson (1985) who attributes to Foot (1967) the appeal to DDA, although she (Thomson) does note (1985: note 4, 1396), correctly, that Foot actually appeals to the distinction between negative duties (to avoid harm) and positive duties (to provide aid), with negative duties being generally the more stringent (see also Section 4.2). Quinn (1989b), on the other hand, appeals to rights. But the difference is slight, since Quinn's rights are the dual of Foot's duties – we have one of Foot's duties (not) to treat people in a certain way if and only if they are one of Quinn's rights (not) to be treated by us in that way[5] (see also Section 4.3). In line with Foot's view, it is typically harder, Quinn claims, to justify violating a negative right (by harming someone) than it is to justify violating a positive right (by failing to give aid). Call this the 'rights interpretation' of DDA.

Quinn claims that 'moral blame for the violation of a right depends very much more on motive and expected harm than on the degree to which the right is defeasible' (Quinn, 1989b: 290), so it might be that, in Rachels's bathtub case, our intuition that the doing-allowing distinction makes no difference is explained by the fact that the two uncles have equally evil motives, even though the second ('allowing') uncle violates a less stringent right, so that the case is not a counterexample to DDA under the rights interpretation. But is there a case in which violating a less stringent right is actually more reprehensible? Here's an example from Quinn (1989b). The police may not enter your home uninvited without special justification – they would violate your right to privacy if they did so. On the one hand, this right is less stringent than your right not to have ordinary members of the public doing the same, since in certain emergencies police officers would be justified in breaking into your home when private citizens would not. On the other hand, though, unjustified break-ins by the police are worse than unjustified break-ins by ordinary citizens.

Thus, it seems, stringency of rights violations and degree of harm or badness need not be correlated: the violation of a less stringent right might be on a par with, or even worse than, the violation of a more stringent one. As well as providing a defence of DDA, if this is correct, it may also make it harder for the consequentialist to co-opt the doctrine.

---

[5] The general form of this duality claim is subject to challenge. First, we have a duty to be charitable, but, it may seem, no one has a right to charity. Ross (1930: 53) discusses this issue, and concludes that we are hesitant to countenance a right to beneficence because our notion of a right, perhaps erroneously, incorporates the thoughts that rights can 'in decency' be claimed, and that 'there is something indecent in the making of a *claim* to beneficence'. Or it might be that each of us has a duty to be beneficent, but not to any specific person, and people have a right to beneficence, but not necessarily to the beneficence of someone in particular. Second, we have a duty towards animals, but if rights must be claimable by the rights holder, then animals have none (see Ross, 1930: 50), and the same holds if rights holders must have 'a moral nature' (Ross, 1930: 52).

It is often assumed that 'consequentialists believe that doing harm is no worse than merely allowing harm' (Woollard and Howard-Snyder, 2021: 1). But this need not be the case: as with DDE, the consequentialist could attempt to draw on whatever arguments the deontologist deploys in favour of DDA to argue that doing is indeed worse (in the consequentialist sense, i.e., more disvaluable) than allowing (in those cases, if any, where it is). However, if DDA is expressed in terms of rights, then the consequentialist will argue, as we have seen, that rights violations are bad, thus we should minimize them, even if that requires violating some of them ourselves (thus, of course, the consequentialist can incorporate only what we might call 'ersatz rights'). And, presumably, the more stringent the right violated (by deontological lights), the worse. But Quinn is suggesting that this last is not true.

The problem for the consequentialist, if Quinn is correct, is that, if her standard argument against rights is to prevail, she must deny that it is always the case that the more stringent the right being violated, the worse, and countenance the counterintuitive possibility that we should, at least on occasion, violate more stringent (ersatz) rights in order to prevent less stringent ones being violated. Now, in revisionist spirit, she may try to shrug this off. But is Quinn correct?

Looking at his example from the deontologist's perspective, it may be that members of the public at large have less of a *legal* right than the police to enter your home uninvited and without justification, since the police have special powers granted by the state. But it is this latter fact, it could be argued, that gives the police less of a *moral* right to enter your home without justification: it is an abuse of their special powers. With police special powers come more stringent moral duties not to harm people without justification, and, correlatively, people have more stringent moral rights not to be harmed by the police. Thus the deontologist *can* appeal to the relative stringency of the moral rights being violated, after all, to explain why violations by the police are more reprehensible than violations by the general public.

The deontological opponent of Quinn can agree, then, that often negative rights (rights not to be harmed) are more stringent than positive ones (rights to aid), but, *pace* Quinn, in those cases the violation of negative rights is always more reprehensible than the violation of positive rights. As regards Rachels's bathtub case, it could be argued that although the two uncles manifest equally bad character, the murdering uncle violates a more stringent right, and hence his behaviour is worse.

And the consequentialist can continue to deploy her standard argument: where the deontologist sees the violation of a more stringent moral right, she sees a worse harm.

But another of Quinn's suggestions may tell against consequentialism. Why do negative rights take precedence over positive? Quinn (1989b: 308–9) claims that this is because our bodies belong to us, and part of what this entails is that we have a moral claim on other people not to harm our bodies against our wishes, even at a greater cost to others in terms of aid that they would not gain as a result. If this is correct, the anti-consequentialist upshot would be that people cannot be sacrificed simply in order to minimize costs.

However, even if Quinn is correct that we should have a say about what happens to our bodies, and that this entails the precedence of negative rights over positive, the consequentialist can still agree (with ersatz rights taking the place of rights proper, of course). Quinn's mistake, if he seeks to challenge consequentialism, is to suppose that the consequentialist must look only at the losses and gains to the various potential victims. As usual, the consequentialist can be more subtle, and, in this case, attribute intrinsic value to people having a say about what happens to their bodies. And then she can mirror the argument to the precedence of negative rights over positive by claiming that the disvalue of being harmed against our wishes outweighs the value of the benefit of comparable, or even greater, aid.

Under what circumstances, then, is the consequentialist disagreement with Quinn made manifest? In an admittedly far-fetched situation in which, by violating one person's negative rights in order to prevent several positive rights' violations, we can prevent many more cases of this same behaviour. And, notes the consequentialist, minimizing this behaviour is the best way, in this circumstance, to make sure that as many people as possible have a say over the disposition of their bodies.

One might attempt to evade this consequentialist strategy by arguing that violating any negative right in order to prevent several comparable positive rights' violations is always wrong. The intuition might be that this claim is a key part of what it means for our bodies to belong to us. The consequentialist, on the other hand, as we have seen, can accommodate only ersatz rights, claiming merely that violating a negative (ersatz) right to prevent positive rights' violations is bad, and thus to be minimized, ceteris paribus. But can the deontologist hold to her hard-line position? It is doubtful. For example, deontologists acknowledge that some rights, even negative ones, are less stringent than others, and thus endorse the violation of the less stringent to prevent violations of the more so. Why would the claim of self-ownership be associated with the inviolability of negative rights only when they are in competition with positive rights, as opposed to other negative rights? And deontologists typically agree that it is permissible, if not obligatory, to harm people if that is the only way to come to the aid of a vastly greater number of people who would otherwise perish in a catastrophe.

Finally, how does DDA fare when we view matters through the lens of normative reasons? The advocate of DDA can be seen as contending that the fact that some act would harm someone is typically a stronger moral reason against doing it than the fact that it would allow harm to befall them. If justification here is a matter of moral reasons, this is just a restatement of the view: that it is harder, morally speaking, to justify doing harm than to allow it. And this may well be the case on some occasions but not others. To take this position requires abandoning DDA's claim to generality, but this latter claim may simply reflect a generalist prejudice (cf Section 6). Furthermore, where there is a difference in reason strength vis-à-vis doing versus allowing, this could reflect only a difference in value, which is, of course, of no help in defending deontology.

As with DDE, there is a vast and complex literature concerning DDA (see Woollard and Howard-Snyder, 2021), and I have merely scratched the surface. But I hope to have established, among other things, at least the plausibility of the claim that a consequentialist, or someone who sympathizes with the consequentialist rejection of constraints and rights, can accommodate, if need be, the intuitions associated with DDE and DDA. (For further discussion relevant to DDA, see Sections 4.2 and 4.5.)

3 W. D. Ross

W. D. Ross[6] endeavoured to systematize our moral intuitions, as he saw them, by proposing a list of prima facie duties. In this section I present this list, and some other features of his view. In the next I discuss more explicitly its deontological aspects.

3.1 Prima Facie Duties

Ross is perhaps best known for his list of prima facie duties (1930: 19–27). These can be thought of as his list of the most fundamental moral considerations, which always count in favour of the acts to which they apply – they are universally (morally) positive. There are seven in Ross's initial list:

1) Keeping promises or commitments (fidelity)
2) Making amends for my wrongdoing (reparation)
3) Benefiting those who have benefited me (gratitude)
4) Distributing benefits and burdens according to merit or desert (justice)
5) Bettering the condition of others (beneficence)
6) Bettering my own condition (self-improvement)
7) Not harming others (non-maleficence).

---

[6] For a recent in-depth discussion of Rossian ethics, see Phillips, 2019.

But he may be seen as shortening it to five (although he does not preclude its lengthening again – he does not claim completeness for the list (1930: 23)). Ross is a pluralist about the good, and he holds that self-improvement, justice, and beneficence reflect its components, so the trio of associated duties 'comes under the general principle that we should produce as much good as possible' (1930: 27). However, this does not rule out each of the trio's being fundamental: they correspond to constituents of the good rather than being grounded in it.

Crucially, these considerations can conflict. For example, you might find yourself in a situation in which by breaking a promise (which would violate the duty of fidelity – that your act would break a promise counts against it) you could act so as to benefit a great many people by preventing a disaster, which counts in that act's favour (in accordance with the duty of beneficence). You are then in the position of assessing which of the duties is more pressing in your circumstance – if, for instance, the promise is relatively trivial, then your course is clear: your moral duty is to prevent the disaster.

As Ross himself points out (1930: 20), the term 'prima facie duties' is misleading, since the items on the list are neither duties proper nor prima facie (in the sense of being based on a first impression that may turn out to be incorrect). They are not duties proper, since we may, for example, have an overall duty to violate them, as in the case of the promise discussed in the previous paragraph. And they are not prima facie, since not only are they not first impressions, but also, even when we are not obligated to follow them, they remain morally relevant. If you break a promise to prevent a disaster, you may still owe something to your promisee, even if just an apology and an explanation.

These fundamental prima facie duties give rise to various derivative duties, such as the duty not to lie. This latter duty 'arises' from the fundamental duties of non-maleficence and fidelity, which ground it and explain its force. Lying normally harms the person lied to, and undermines an implicit undertaking to tell the truth (1930: 54–5). But such explanations cannot go on forever. Eventually we reach the bedrock of fundamental duties; here we cannot appeal to anything more basic to explain why the features they mention are morally significant.

Furthermore, Ross thinks that the fundamental prima facie duties, in virtue of being fundamental, are universally morally positive, whereas derivative prima facie duties may not be: they may lose their moral force in the absence of the fundamental features that ground them elsewhere. Ross holds, for instance, that the implicit undertaking not to lie is lessened if I am a complete stranger in another society, and have had no chance to reach agreements of any sort with its members. Since he sees a large part of our duty not to lie as stemming from the supposed implicit promise, its absence greatly weakens our duty not to lie.

Although Ross does not discuss this point, it seems perfectly possible that there might be cases where *none* of the considerations that normally tell against lying apply. If we are playing a game like Cheat, in which lying is expected, and part of the fun, then we have all agreed to suspend the normal conventions about truth-telling, so that lying may not even be prima facie wrong here since in this instance it violates neither the duty of fidelity nor of non-maleficence. While being in breach of a fundamental prima facie duty always counts against an act, according to Ross, then, being in breach of a derivative duty may not.

Is this true of all derivative duties? Maybe not. Take the duty to pay one's debts. It seems that you can be indebted only in one of two ways: either you have borrowed something on the understanding that you will pay it back or someone has done you a good turn. So perhaps being indebted will always be morally relevant, but, because the duty to pay debts always falls under the fundamental duties of either fidelity or gratitude, it itself is not fundamental. (Henceforth, I shall refer to the fundamental prima facie duties as simply prima facie duties.)

I turn now to the question of how we know that the items on Ross's list belong there – for example, how do we know that it is always the case that violating fidelity counts against an act?

3.2 Ross's Epistemology

In developing his moral theory, Ross employs what came later to be called the method of reflective equilibrium (see Daniels, 2020). We look both at our intuitions about particular cases, and also at plausible general principles. Where they conflict about what we ought to do, we make adjustments to each until they are in accord with each other. But, according to Ross, our reflective judgements about particular cases are to have the final say. We do, of course, form snap judgements about particular cases, and we may revise these in the light not only of judgements about other cases, but also in the light of plausible principles. If, however, after careful reflection, our judgement about a particular case remains at odds with the principles, it is the latter that must give way. If, for example, consequentialism tells us that

> we should give up our view that there is a special obligatoriness attaching to the keeping of promises because it is self-evident that the only duty is to produce as much good as possible, we have to ask ourselves whether we really, when we reflect, *are* convinced that this is self-evident, and whether we really *can* get rid of our view that promise-keeping has a bindingness independent of productiveness of maximum good. . . . [T]o ask us to give up at the bidding of a theory our actual apprehension of what is right and what is

wrong seems like asking people to repudiate their actual experience of beauty, at the bidding of a theory which says 'only that which satisfies such and such conditions can be beautiful'. (1930: 39–40)

So, what is the nature of this 'actual apprehension', and in what cases can we have moral knowledge?

3.3 Certainty and Probable Opinion

Ross draws a sharp distinction between 'our apprehension of the prima facie rightness of certain types' of action (1930: 29) and our judgement about the overall obligatoriness or wrongness of particular acts. That the prima facie duties hold is, Ross claims, self-evident. That an act is, for example, prima facie required in virtue of falling under the duty of justice is something that we can know a priori, by reflection – and it is something of which we can be (relatively) certain. By contrast, about what we should do – what is overall required – in some particular case we can only form what Ross calls a 'probable opinion'.

One reason for this is that there are nearly always morally relevant considerations for and against any act (and even when we don't think there are, we cannot be sure). To decide what to do, we have to balance those considerations, and that calls for the exercise of judgement – there is no algorithm for determining which of our prima facie duties are the weightiest in any given case.

Another reason is that we can never know enough about our circumstance or its future to know the degree to which we are succeeding (if at all) in our endeavours to, say, fulfil the duty of beneficence: what you think is of benefit to someone may turn out not to be.

3.4 Self-evidence and the Heterogeneity of the Prima Facie Duties

Ross claims that the (fundamental) prima facie principles can, as noted, be known with certainty. But how? Initially, we may accept that we should, say, keep our promises on the basis of authority. But, as we mature and reflect upon our judgements in various cases concerning promise-keeping, we can come to see for ourselves that we have a prima facie duty to keep them (see Ross, 1939: 170–3). That we have such a duty is a self-evident truth – it requires no proof. Rather, one can justifiably believe a self-evident truth on the basis of simply understanding it (see Audi, 1996: 114).

What is self-evident need not be *obvious*. Such propositions are evident to those with sufficient mental abilities and experience who have reflected properly about them. Ross's analogy here is with our knowledge of mathematical axioms and forms of inference. The fundamental principles of mathematics, logic, and ethics are not *analytic*; that is, they are not true in virtue of the meanings of the terms employed in them. They are, thinks Ross, synthetic propositions that can be known a priori. Whether and how there can be synthetic a priori knowledge is a contentious issue,[7] but note that Ross is *not* claiming that moral principles are known by some special faculty, as his detractors sometimes suppose (see Mackie, 1977, and also Audi, 1996).

There are, of course, many differences among mathematics, logic, and ethics. But they have this in common: their fundamental propositions are not susceptible to empirical justification – a feature they share with philosophy, and, indeed, in part, empirical science itself: the scientific method cannot be assessed scientifically, since that would require following the method, and thus beg the question. The idea, then, is that these fundamental propositions can neither be verified empirically nor derived from anything more basic. If they are known, it must be through reflection on their contents: they are self-evident. Ross is here placing himself squarely in a mainstream philosophical tradition that holds there are substantial claims, including ethical ones, whose truth we can know by direct rational insight.

Is this correct? Robert Audi suggests that Ross sometimes expresses himself in ways that make his claim sound stronger, and thus less plausible, than it need be. It is not, for example, necessary in order to apprehend the truth of a proposition that is self-evident, that one also recognize that it is self-evident (Audi, 1996: 106). Nor should we follow Ross in claiming that we can be certain of the general principles of duty if by that he meant that we could not be mistaken about them. Further reflection on what seems self-evident can lead to a change of mind. In the case of promising, for example, do we have any reason to keep a promise that was extracted under duress? Perhaps we need a more nuanced account of fidelity, so that not all promises fall under it (see Ross, 1939, chapter five for relevant discussion).

As Audi further points out (1996: 117), Ross also makes a stronger claim than needed in claiming not only that self-evident principles need no proof, but also that they cannot be proved. Though we can know them without evidence, this does not mean that there could be no further evidence for them. Insofar as a Kantian agrees with the list, for example, she would presumably propose deriving it from the CI (see, e.g., Audi, 2004). However, quite apart from any problems there may be with derivation, difficulties with the CI were suggested in Section 1.5. In Section 4.6, we shall see that the rule consequentialist suggests the good as fulfilling the role, but it too misses the mark, or so I shall argue.

---

[7] But there are, of course, many potential examples of it, such as the knowledge that nothing can be both red and white all over.

If either of these strategies were to succeed, however, they would address a complaint made by some that Ross's list lacks the unity desirable in a theory because the basic duties are not connected to each other. But, if Ross is correct, then his list is unified by the fact that its items are right-making features of acts. And why need there be any commonality beyond this?

The consequentialist, however, might claim the advantage of unity for her theory with its single duty to maximize the good. But unless she is a monist about value, she will propose a list of goods against which any complaint of heterogeneity can also be made. And arriving at the list of goods poses the same difficulties as arriving at a list of deontological duties. In Ross's view, the 'list of goods put forward by the [consequentialist] is reached by exactly the same method [as Ross uses to compile his list of duties] – the only sound one in the circumstances – viz. that of direct reflection on what we really think' (1930: 23).

3.5 The Role of the Prima Facie Duties

The prima facie duties clearly play a classificatory role – acts can be classified as harmful or beneficent, as the keeping of a promise, or the repayment of a debt of gratitude. But do they play a larger role than this? In particular, do they help guide us in determining our moral obligations? Ross thinks that, in general, they don't. While there may be special circumstances in which we have to consult the list of duties in order to see what we have moral reason to do, on most occasions we can see directly the moral pros and cons of any proposed course of action. (And, as already mentioned, of course, judgement is then required to assess what is required of us overall.) It is, then, on Ross's view, true that we have the prima facie duties we do, but their chief role may be merely classificatory, at least to those who have internalized them.

4 Ross, Deontology, and Its Defence against Consequentialism

In this section, I discuss the extent to which Ross's view incorporates the four elements of what might be dubbed 'full-blown' deontology: constraints, duties of special obligation, options, and a requirement to do some good. And, in the course of doing so, I shall explore the defence of deontology against consequentialism.

4.1 Duties of Special Obligation

As noted in Section 3.1, three duties on Ross's list of seven can be subsumed under the prima facie duty to do good. So it is to the other four that we need to turn for the aspects of his view that conflict most directly with consequential-ism. Of these four, three, namely, the prima facie duties of fidelity, reparation, and gratitude, are duties of special obligation. In each case the duty rests on some previous act(s), either of my own or of others, that has (have) contributed to a relationship between us. It is because of this relationship that the other person has a claim on me to a benefit, and often to a very specific benefit. Others who don't stand in these relationships do not have these claims.

Ross says the following:

> The essential defect of [consequentialism] is that it ignores, or at least does not do full justice to, the highly personal character of duty. If the only duty is to produce the maximum of good, the question who is to have the good – whether it is myself, or my benefactor, or a person to whom I have made a promise to confer that good on him, or a mere fellow man to whom I stand in no such special relation – should make no difference to my having a duty to produce that good. But we are all in fact sure that it makes a vast difference. (1930: 22)

Ross holds not only that, given a choice, I should benefit my benefactor, or the person to whom I have made a promise, rather than a stranger, but that I should do so even if I could benefit the stranger slightly more at no extra cost to myself or others:

> Suppose ... the fulfilment of a promise to A would produce 1,000 units of good for him, but that by doing some other act I could produce 1,001 units of good for B, to whom I have made no promise, the other consequences of the two acts being of equal value. (1930: 34–5)

In such a case we would, Ross claims, believe we should keep our promise. If we are right in this belief, he holds, consequentialism must be false, since we ought to produce the state that has less value.

But Ross's reasoning here is flawed. He is assuming that, when we compare the value of two states of affairs, we need only consider the size of the benefits to all individuals. So the state that contains more benefits will contain more value. But consequentialism need not assume this, as Ross should know. For, on his own account of justice, a state of affairs in which benefits are distributed according to desert is more valuable than one where the same amount of benefit is not so distributed. It is crucial to distinguish between benefits, or well-being, on the one hand, and value, or the good, on the other (see also Section 1.4). To conflate the two not only undermines Ross's own account of justice, but also commits the consequentialist to some version of welfarist utilitarianism according to which well-being is the only good, so we must maximize its total sum. This leads to many well-known difficulties, such as the possibility of endorsing a society in which the sum of well-being is maximized at the expense of having a few desperate people (such as slaves) who ensure that the majority live well, or of viewing a society in which many people live lives just worth living as better than one in which far fewer people live much better lives because the total sum of welfare in the former is greater (Parfit's (1984) 'repugnant conclusion'; see also Broad, 1930: 249–50; Ross, 1939: 69–71).[8]

A more persuasive consequentialist view maintains that acts of promise-keeping, gratitude, and reparation are themselves valuable (see Section 1.4). In that case, the total value of keeping the promise to A will be the sum of the value that comes from A's receiving those benefits, plus the value of promise-keeping itself – in which case, keeping the promise to A might well produce more value than giving a slightly larger benefit to B. Ross seems to suppose that providing x units of welfare to someone (i.e., x units of good *for* them) produces x units of good simpliciter. But the consequentialist can deny this and claim that units of welfare are independent of units of good. She might, for instance, hold the following view of Ross's example: keeping the promise to A has value x; providing 1,000 units of welfare to A has value y; and providing 1,001 units of welfare to B has value z. She then asks which is greater: $x + y$ or z? And the answer is determined by the particulars of the case.

In reply, the Rossian could concede this point and still maintain that consequentialism is mistaken both about the strength and the nature of duties of special obligation. If I have promised to pay back the money I have borrowed, but instead donate the money to charity, many people would think I acted wrongly, even if I brought about more good by breaking my promise. Or suppose I successfully encourage other people to keep their promises, so that a few more promises are kept overall, but at the expense of my not keeping my own. Even here it seems implausible to claim, as consequentialism would, that to keep my own promises would be wrong.

It might be argued that consequentialism underestimates the strength of duties of special relationship because it misunderstands their nature. As well as any general duty I may have to encourage acts of promise-keeping, I also have a specific duty *to my promisee* to keep my promise, a duty whose strength is disproportionate to the value of my keeping my promise. The consequentialist claims that I should adopt a policy of keeping my promises, but only because such acts tend to make the world a better place. The deontologist responds: it is not just that the world is better for people honouring their commitments; the people to whom we are committed have special claims on us.

Consider friendship, and our commitments and duties to our friends, such as loyalty. Here the consequentialist might respond to Ross's claim that the 'essential defect of [consequentialism] is that it ignores, or at least does not

---

[8] Note also that the consequentialist need not be committed to thinking that the value of a person is to be equated to her welfare. And neither need the consequentialist be committed to the view that a state is made more valuable by having more valuable things in it: that people are valuable, for example, need not entail that the state of the world is improved by an increase in their number.

do full justice to, the highly personal character of duty' by asserting that such loyalty is itself valuable. So we should each ensure that, ceteris paribus, everyone is loyal to their friends. Thus, if, by being disloyal to our own friends, we could ensure more loyalty overall, this should be our course. Generally speaking, no one's friendships are any more valuable than anyone else's, no one's betrayals are any worse than anyone else's, and consequentialism can claim to capture these facts. Furthermore, since friendship is valuable, friends benefiting friends is to be promoted, since such behaviour in turn promotes the good of friendship. Consequentialism can claim, then, to explain why we should favour our friends by appealing to the value of friendship.

Consequentialism, on this approach, entails that if, by betraying your friends yourself, you could ensure that more friends are loyal to one another, you should betray your friends. The deontologist, on the other hand, maintains that, while perhaps we should promote loyalty among friends, we should not do so at the expense of betraying our own.

In general, the consequentialist would have us promote friendship, even at the expense of abandoning our own friends. In these divisive times, suppose the government sets up an agency to promote friendship, and you have the opportunity to head it up. But it proves to be immensely time-consuming – so much so that you would have to abandon your friends to continue in the role. But it's going swimmingly: friendships across the nation are blossoming. Consequentialism, then, is likely to come down on the side of your continuing, whereas deontology is likely to prescribe that you quit.

The deontologist's view is that there is more to friendship than its value. I have *special* duties to my friends that I don't owe to strangers. I have *special* reasons to benefit my friends that I don't have to benefit strangers. And, crucially, the strengths of these special duties and reasons are greater than the mere value of my acting upon them would warrant. That I have such special duties towards, and reasons to favour, my friends is partly constitutive of friendship. If the strength of my reason to benefit my friend were dictated only by the impartial value of my benefiting her, then my reason to benefit her would not result from the fact that she is special in my eyes. Rather, it would be that doing so makes the world a better place. She would merely be, as it were, a repository for the bounty of my value-maximizing efforts. And this would rule out friendship.

Or consider love relationships. The consequentialist could attempt to accommodate them by appealing to their value. But imagine discovering that your romantic partner showers you with affection only because they think that love relationships are good, and that showering you with affection is the best way to promote such relationships (at least for today).

Friendship develops over time, and thus has an historical component. But perhaps consequentialism can accommodate such history by viewing states of the world as histories (see Section 1.4). However, the deontologist maintains, consequentialism cannot do the same for the special bonds between friends. This is not to say that acts of friendship are inconsistent with consequentialism, but, if we were to follow the doctrine, we would be required to break any bonds that developed whenever the greater good beckoned. And that is inconsistent with their being bonds of friendship.

Given, then, that friendship requires that we stick by our friends, and benefit them, to a greater degree than the value of such behaviour prescribes, consequentialism cannot accommodate friendship. And this, in turn, undercuts the consequentialist claim that friendship is valuable, and that we should benefit our friends – if consequentialism rules out friendship, it cannot claim it as something valuable, and there can be no friends to benefit. (The same thoughts apply to love, of course, mutatis mutandis.)

How might the consequentialist respond? She might point out that, even if there is no such thing as friendship as envisaged by the deontologist (there being no reasons to benefit anyone beyond the value of doing so), nevertheless consequentialism can accommodate bonhomie as part of the good (and thus advocate that we promote it). The deontologist's concern, of course, is that mere bonhomie does not suffice for friendship: on the consequentialist picture we could, claims the deontologist, at best have a mere imitation of friendship. But the consequentialist could go on to claim that it may be best, then, if we harbour false beliefs to the effect that we really do have special reasons to benefit our friends. After all, what matters, it might be claimed, is that our friends hold us in special esteem, whether or not they have reason to do so.

The same thought might be applied to promising: perhaps the institution would disappear if we all thought that a promise should be broken whenever the greater good beckoned. But, if so, what would then be key is that we continue to believe otherwise: it would be better if we persisted in our false (by consequentialist lights) belief that we have stronger reason to keep our promises than the value of doing so warrants.

On this approach, consequentialism would be in part self-effacing: as regards special relationships, things would go best if we did not believe it. This would place the consequentialist in an awkward position, to say the least. For instance, she might find herself having to argue for deontology in order to conceal the truth. Furthermore, perhaps knowledge and true beliefs are themselves valuable – Ross certainly thought so: it 'seems clear that knowledge, and in a less degree ... "right opinion", are states of mind good in themselves' (1930: 138–9).

Ross, however, as we have seen, speaks of *duties* of special obligation, and this raises concerns about how well deontology itself can accommodate friendship and love. Always acting out of duty towards one's friends and loved ones seems, at best, inappropriate. But the deontologist can respond that there is a distinction between having a duty and acting from it. We have seen an analogous response (see Section 1.2) to the worry that, in responding to those reasons to favour friends and family that are classified as moral, we must be motivated by a sense of obligation. One deontological line, then, is that we have duties towards friends, or moral reasons to treat them in certain ways, and are aware of this, but in fulfilling these duties, or acting on these moral reasons, we need not always do so out of 'moral' motives. I have a duty (or moral reason) to visit my friend in hospital, as I do to visit an unpleasant and irritating relative. In the second case, I might have to summon up my sense of duty, but, in the first, I might visit purely out of affection. Ross himself denies that it is ever our duty to act from a certain motive (1930: 4–6). So he certainly rejects the view that in fulfilling a duty of special relationship we must act out of a sense of duty.

4.2 Constraints

The remaining duty on Ross's list is that of non-maleficence, the prima facie duty not to harm. Can consequentialism accommodate it? It depends on how we understand it, and here Ross is somewhat unclear. He claims that it is wrong to inflict harm on someone in order to produce a similar, or slightly larger, benefit for someone else. (This is related to the doctrine of doing and allowing: see Section 2.2.) But this might be because bringing about a harm of a certain sort produces more disvalue than failing to give a benefit of a similar sort. Generally speaking, taking away something someone already has seems worse than failing to give her that thing when she lacks it. If that is so, then consequentialism can accommodate the thought by simply recognizing the greater disvalue in depriving someone of an existing benefit.

But does Ross agree with this, or does he, rather, think that there is a threshold constraint against harming? Unlike duties of special relationship, constraints (see Section 1.1) require us not harm *anyone*, including strangers, in various ways. Ross certainly does not argue that there are absolute constraints, since these would forbid you to inflict the harm whatever the circumstance, which would not comport with his claim that our duties are prima facie in his sense. But it is consistent with his view that there be threshold constraints, in the form of finite constraining reasons (see Section 1.2), so that there could be circumstances in which you should not harm someone even though it would maximize the good to do so. Indeed, Ross does not list non-maleficence under the umbrella of value, so this is not an unreasonable interpretation, albeit an anachronistic one. However, Ross does not propose a defence of constraints against the consequentialist. So how might they be defended?

I shall largely focus on constraints against certain intentional harms, such as intentionally killing the innocent. Some deontologists see constraints as prohibitions on certain intentions, others as prohibitions on certain harms, intentional or not. These alternatives yield different prescriptions in certain cases, but the basic consequentialist argument against constraints applies to all three: what is so special about your agency that *you* are barred from doing certain things, or forming certain intentions, or both, *yourself*, as opposed to minimizing the bad intentions or actions, even at the expense of your violating the constraints?

Consider, for example, a tragic case in which a mobster threatens that unless you (intentionally) kill some innocent woman, he will kill her and her child. There are no other alternatives, and you know this, so what should you do? The consequentialist might well require you to kill. The advocate of an absolute constraint against killing the innocent would require you not to. This is a particularly troublesome case for the deontologist, of course, because the woman will be killed in either case.

But perhaps the deontologist might modify the constraint to claim that it is only if you will harm them by doing so that you must not kill the innocent. And then the claim could be that, since the woman will be killed by the mobster if you do not do it, your killing her will not harm her. However, this modification would not work in a more standard case in which, unless you kill one, the mobster will kill several others.

Alternatively, the advocate of a threshold constraint against killing the innocent might claim that in this case the threshold would be met, and your killing the woman is permissible. But advocates of a threshold constraint typically set the bar higher than a net saving of one. And wherever the bar is set, there will be cases in which you are barred from violating a constraint even though your violating it would be better in terms of value (otherwise there would be no constraints).

Another difficulty for constraints is raised by Jackson and Smith (2006). They consider a case in which you are uncertain as to whether a potential target is an innocent. Suppose you are faced with a circumstance in which by killing one person you can save several others from being killed by other agents, but you believe there is a constraint against killing the one if he is innocent, something of which you are unsure. One thought is that the deontologist might propose a credence threshold: if you have a reasonable credence of, say, at least 70 per cent that your potential target is a mobster, then you ought to kill him, but otherwise killing him is impermissible. Jackson and Smith point out that this will lead to problems if you are faced with parallel independent cases. Suppose by pushing the left button you can kill A and save five, and by pushing the right button you can kill B and save a different five, where your credence that A is a mobster is 70 per cent, and similarly for B. Furthermore, your credence that A is a mobster given that B is a mobster is also 70 per cent (the propositions are probabilistically independent for you). Then your credence that A and B are both mobsters should be, by probability theory, 49 per cent. So apparently you ought to kill A and you ought to kill B, but you are barred from killing A and B.

And there are other difficulties. One is the issue of what makes a credence reasonable. Another (pointed out to me by Marshall Bierson) is that, in a case in which you have other motives to kill someone, you might bias your information gathering in order to increase your credence that he is a mobster.

Despite these difficulties, constraints seem to be widely accepted, so I shall now address some of the attempts to provide a rationale for them. But my view is that none of these succeed. At best they fall back on the basic thought that you simply should not do certain things, even in the pursuit of good ends, but this is just to reiterate that there are constraints. However, constraints can be made part of a deontology without introducing contradiction, so their inclusion or not is, I think, simply a bedrock matter.

One defence of constraints might tackle the consequentialist complaint head-on, and agree that each of us benefits by keeping our own hands clean by not violating constraints ourselves (see Dreier, 2011: 118). Violating constraints is a nasty business that leaves emotional scars, for example, so we should not violate them. But this is hardly the moral defence that advocates of constraints seek.

Alternatively, one might try an Aristotelian approach: virtuous activity is beneficial to the those who engage in it, adhering to constraints is virtuous, thus adhering to constraints is beneficial to those who adhere to them, and so adherence is warranted. However, this presupposes that adhering to constraints is virtuous, which begs the question against the consequentialist who maintains, rather, that it is minimizing harm that is virtuous.

The same difficulty besets those who defend constraints by arguing that, in violating a constraint, you are 'setting yourself at evil', which we are forbidden to do (see Aquinas's *Summa Theologica*). The consequentialist simply denies that intentionally violating a constraint in order to do *good* involves setting yourself at evil.

Another defence denies that one can sum up constraint violations in the manner proposed by the consequentialist – two violations are in some sense no worse than one. But now suppose you can, without doing harm yourself, prevent one violation or two – surely you should prevent the two. (Taurek, 1977, might deny this under certain circumstances.)

There is another class of defences that, I contend, all implicitly presuppose a relationship between the violator and the violated. Thus these defences are either not defences of constraints, but, rather (insofar as they succeed), defences of certain duties of special obligation, or it turns out that the relationship holds between us all, in which case we are back to square one. I cannot, of course, address all such defences, but Darwall's Kantian appeal to second-personal reasons is a prominent example.

A 'second-personal reason' is

> a distinctive kind of reason for acting . . . that, to exist at all, must be able to be *addressed* second-personally ('I' or 'we' or 'you') by free and rational agents to other agents. (Darwall, 2006: 305)

By way of illustration, Darwall (2006: 307) contrasts 'two different ways in which you might try to give someone [a stranger, we'll assume] a reason to stop causing you pain, say, to remove his foot from on top of yours'. One way would be to try and persuade him that pain is bad, and that removing his foot will improve the state of the world – the consequentialist strategy. The other, deontological, strategy would be to

> insist that the other move his foot as a way of advancing a valid demand, from one equal member of the moral community to another, that he stop *causing* you pain. This would address a second-personal reason that presumes on your equal authority as members of the moral community to demand that people not step on one another's feet. Here the reason would be agent-relative, addressed distinctively to the person causing another pain rather than impli-citly to anyone who might be in a position to relieve it. . . . [This] reason would purport . . . to be independent of the agent-neutral value of outcomes.

These two strategies differ not only in their rationales, but also in their practical upshots. On the consequentialist approach, the idea is that treading on others' feet is bad, and should be minimized. According to the deontologist, by contrast, each of us should avoid stepping on others' feet ourselves. If (in admittedly unlikely circumstances) by treading on a stranger's foot I could prevent several people from treading on further strangers' feet, then the consequentialist might have me do it, whereas the deontologist would not.

But what is Darwall's case for the existence of second-personal reasons – that is, for the claim that second-personal demands and claims are normatively authoritative for rational agents (and, indeed, are the only claims and demands that possess this property)? It apparently hinges on the idea that even strangers are in a certain kind of relationship – one that is a necessary condition of the very possibility of second-personal demands having normative authority: '[m]aking and entertaining demands and claims second-personally at all is *already* to be in a relation in which each reciprocally recognizes the other and gives him an authority as a free and rational person' (2006: 310).

Rather than being an argument for the normative status of second-personal demands, however, this seems to presuppose it: the starting assumption appears to be that we are all in the relevant normative authority-conferring relationships. And there is a further difficulty. In the unlikely case above in which I'm treading on one stranger's foot to prevent others from treading on further strangers' feet, why does my 'relationship' with the first stranger take precedence over the other potential treaders', and my own, 'relationships' with those strangers whose feet I am protecting? Given Darwall's emphasis above on the demand that the treader 'stop *causing* you pain', perhaps the idea is that it is the direct causal nature of my relationship to the pain of the stranger on whose foot I am treading that accounts for this. But, of course, we need to be told what counts as direct causation of harm, why it makes such a difference, and, most pressingly, why it should not be minimized. We are back to square one: by directly causing you pain, I can prevent several others directly causing pain, so what is so special about my agency and my relation to you? Why should I not maximize the meeting of potential demands to get off toes, rather than merely meeting your demand to me?

4.3 The Patient-Centred Approach: Constraints and Rights

So far deontology has largely been characterized as an agent-relative moral theory, in contrast to agent-neutral consequentialism. In particular, constraints have been portrayed as focused on the role of each of us as agents: we are told that we should not perform certain kinds of acts, even to prevent others from doing more of the same. The account we have given so far might, then, be characterized as agent-focused, which is what leads to the complaint of narcissism: each of us should apparently keep our own hands clean rather than minimize the number of dirty hands. But there is an alternative approach that sees rights, rather than constraints, as fundamental.

According to this alternative, we should look to the inviolable status of the potential victim (or 'patient'), embodied in her rights. And this, some claim, renders deontology more defensible against consequentialism. The rights in question are the duals of duties not to violate constraints, where, on this approach, constraints are metaphysically dependent on rights: when there is a constraint against my treating you in a certain way, this is because you have a right not to be so treated by me. When it comes to what you should do, the difference in focus between the two deontological accounts becomes evident when rights are going to be violated.

Suppose we have a right not to be physically harmed by others, and a right to our possessions. Now suppose further that a criminal gang threatens both to cut off Victor's thumbs *and* steal all his possessions, unless you cut off his thumbs. On a patient-focused version of deontology, it may be that you should cut off his thumbs, thereby minimizing the violation of his rights overall, by violating one of them yourself. But, on the agent-focused version, you should be centrally concerned with avoiding rights violations *yourself*, and so you shouldn't cut off Victor's thumbs. On the other hand, suppose you've planted a bomb that will kill several innocents, but now regret it. And suppose further that the only way to save these innocents involves your killing some further innocent. The patient-focused version of deontology might forbid this, by claiming that the unthreatened further innocent's right to life trumps the right to life of those already under threat. The agent-focused version, on the other hand, might have you minimize your own constraint violations, and bid you do it (so that you would only commit one constraint violation instead of several).

There is a constraint against cutting thumbs off and bombing; we have a right to our thumbs and a right not to be bombed. But these rights are going to be violated in the aforementioned examples. And then the question is which should have greater force: your concern with your own agency, or, in the first case, minimizing the violation of a given person's rights, even if that requires violating one of their rights yourself?

All deontologists might agree that we have inviolable status: our rights should not be violated. The issue is how we should respond to that inviolability when someone's rights are about to be violated. The advocate of an agent-focused deontology contends that you should not do any violating yourself, unless perhaps to minimize your own violations. The advocate of a patient-focused deontology contends that you should not violate anyone's rights, unless perhaps you can thereby minimize the violations of *that person's* rights. Consequentialism takes it a step further, and asks why the minimization should apply only intra-personally: what if, by violating some right once yourself, you can prevent many more violations of that same right? Surely, says the consequentialist, you should do it, regardless of whether the violations are going to involve one victim or many.

At best (from the deontologist's perspective), then, consequentialism incorporates ersatz rights. The consequentialist can maintain that certain kinds of harms (those seen by the deontologist as rights violations) are particularly bad, and that bad should be minimized, even if that requires inflicting some of the bad harms.

Are rights more defensible than constraints? Consider a case in which killing someone yourself is the only way to prevent several killings of other victims by other agents. The advocate of constraints maintains that you should keep your hands clean, and not kill. The advocate of rights says that you should not violate the right to life of your potential victim. From the consequentialist perspective, both accounts wrongly privilege both *your* agency and the rights of *your* potential victim. No progress has been made. Rights or constraints can be incorporated as a primitive in a deontology, but neither is more defensible than the other if what is desired is an appeal to something more basic than both.

The final argument concerning constraints that I shall consider concludes that there can be no options without constraints. So I turn now to the topic of options.

4.4 Options

Ross is opposed to consequentialism insofar as he believes that there are duties of reparation, gratitude, fidelity, and non-maleficence (if interpreted as incorporating constraining reasons), since these duties may conflict with the prima facie duty to maximize the good. However, this latter duty leaves Ross open to some of the criticisms that have been levelled against consequentialism.

As we saw in Section 2.1, deontology (in agreement with common-sense morality) standardly incorporates *options* – the permission to pursue personal projects or have some fun, provided we fulfil our duties, including doing a certain amount of good. But Ross denies options a place: where no other duties are incumbent upon us, he holds that we should produce as much good as we can, so there is always some duty in need of immediate fulfillment. This makes the morality he advocates, like consequentialism, very pervasive and demanding, with no room for supererogation (see Section 1.1). Thus his theory is in conflict with normal reflective ethical thought (see Wiggins, 1998; Dancy, 1998; Darwall, 1998).

For Ross, the only consideration that can outweigh one prima facie duty is another one. But that is doubtful. One can on occasion have good reasons not to fulfil a prima facie duty which are not themselves reasons of duty. I promised to mark this student's essay by tomorrow. I'm very tired and nothing disastrous will happen if I am a day late. These are good reasons to go to bed rather than mark the essay. But should we think of them as constituting a duty to go to bed, one that is weightier than any duty I have to the student? That seems excessively moralistic. Surely, rather, given that I am not required to keep my promise here, I have the option to go to bed.

This is a genuine worry about Ross's system, but easily accommodated by a friendly amendment. If we distinguish between moral reasons and other types, we can allow the possibility of a non-moral reason being morally relevant, as in

Section 1.2. My tiredness is a reason not to grade the essay, and, despite its not being a moral reason, it can win out.

4.5 Options without Constraints

In Section 4.1, in opposition to consequentialism, duties of special obligation were defended: we may have more reason, say, to benefit our friends than is warranted by the value of doing so. In Section 4.2, in agreement with consequentialism, constraints were subjected to challenge. And in Section 4.3, it was argued that endorsing rights does not help: they are subject to a parallel challenge. Finally, in Section 4.4, a defence of options was proposed. This, if successful, has the consequence that we can have special reasons to benefit ourselves (I will call such reasons 'personal'), in the sense that we can have more reason to do so than consequentialism would allow. Regarding Ross, we have seen along the way that he argued in favour of duties of special obligation, that it is unclear whether he endorsed constraints, but that he did not endorse options. Assuming he did not endorse constraints, however, the only major departure from his position in the account that I am developing here is the endorsement of options, and the related claim that duty can be outweighed by non-moral reasons.

My account, then, includes duties of special obligation and options, but lacks constraints. Some people find constraints hard to drop, however, and I am not denying that they can, without incoherence, be included as a primitive. It is just that attempts to justify them on more basic grounds do not, in my view, succeed. But there may be another justification of constraints in the offing: Kagan (1984) argues that admitting options without constraints leads to counterintuitive consequences (see also Scheffler, 1988, 1994). It is this concern that I will address in this section.

Here is a modification of an example due to Kagan. Suppose there is an option to forgo saving the life of a stranger if it will cost you $10,000. Then why are you not permitted to kill a stranger to gain $10,000?[9] The former permission seems reasonable, but the latter is not. Thus it might appear that endorsing the option requires imposing a constraint against killing.

If one notes that it is not a constraint against killing simpliciter that is required, but an acceptable ban against killing for personal gain, one must face the issue of why there is not also an acceptable ban against refusing to save the life of a stranger to avoid personal cost. How can Kagan's opponent argue that one can refuse to save in order to avoid cost, whereas one cannot kill in order to gain?

---

[9] Kagan's (1984) original example contrasts saving a stranger with killing one's uncle. I have modified it to avoid considerations of special relationships.

There are at least two potentially relevant differences (whether they are actually relevant depends upon the circumstances) that support this.[10] First, killing may be in itself worse than not saving (cf the DDA – see Section 2.2). Second, there may be a morally relevant difference between giving up something of significance to you and not gaining it.

Additionally, in cases of killing, you would usually be solely responsible, whereas, in cases of not saving, you would typically share responsibility with all the others who could have contributed but didn't. Where you would not share responsibility, and there are no other morally significant differences between the killing and the refusal to save, there may well be no option not to save. Rachels's bathtub case (see Section 2.2) may be a case in point. Or suppose that someone is mistakenly taking a valuable antique of yours to the dump, and you are rushing to prevent them. If you delay, you know you will lose it. In the first case, you must stop if you are not to kill a stranger lying unconscious in the road. In the second case, you are the only person capable of saving a stranger from being killed by an oncoming vehicle, but you must stop if you are to do it. It seems you must stop in both cases. But can the advocate of options without constraints agree? Yes. The fact that you are the *only* person capable of saving this life is a crucial morally relevant consideration in the second case: it lessens the difference between harming and failing to prevent harm. But to conclude from this that such a difference is never significant is to overgeneralize.

A theory with special obligations and options, but without constraints, is still deontological in that it sees some agent-relative moral considerations as having priority (your caring for your own family, say, ordinarily takes precedence over trying to aid other people in taking care of theirs), and thus agents are forbidden in certain circumstances to maximize the good, as well as being (merely) permitted not to do so in others. Such a theory disagrees with Ross's since his does not include options, and may include a (threshold) constraint against harm. However, two of the most important features of Ross's view are its rejection of consequentialism, and its inclusion of only prima facie duties. And, provided all its duties are prima facie, a theory with special obligations and options, but without constraints, meets these criteria.

4.6 The Rejection of Rule Consequentialism

So far the discussion of consequentialism has focused upon a version of *act* consequentialism, according to which we have one moral duty: to maximize the good with each act. But there are other versions, one of which, rule

---

[10] For a different view, see Kagan (1989).

consequentialism, might appear to be rather close to Ross's view, at least in the acts it requires. According to this form of consequentialism:

> An act is wrong if and only if it is forbidden by the code of rules whose internalization by the overwhelming majority of everyone everywhere in each new generation has maximum expected value in terms of well-being (with some priority for the worst off). The calculation of a code's expected value includes all costs of getting the code internalized. If in terms of expected value two or more codes are better than the rest but equal to one another, the one closest to conventional morality determines what acts are wrong. (Hooker, 2000: 32)

It may be that the rules that make up the proposed code are fairly similar in content to Ross's prima facie duties (see Hooker, 2000: 107). And, assuming that this is the case, rule consequentialism might seem to have an advantage over Rossian deontology: its rules have an underlying, and unifying, justification that Ross's account lacks – namely that, from among the feasible sets of rules, a set is selected that would maximize expected value if internalized (see Hooker, 2000: 107). But this purported advantage might be outweighed by the various problems facing rule consequentialism.

One standard challenge runs as follows. One goal of rule consequentialism is the maximization of the good (in the form of expected value). But the rules must be simple enough for everyone to internalize, and so it is not hard to imagine a circumstance in which someone works out how to do better, in terms of expected value, by not following such simple rules. Yet the rule consequentialist would have her follow the rules. This is a difficulty, however, only if rule consequentialism claims that following its rules will maximize value (since we are imagining a case in which it will not). But this may not be the case. Here is what Hooker (2000: 101) has to say:

> Most philosophers seem convinced that defending rule-consequentialism is a lost cause once one accepts an overarching commitment to maximize the good. Suppose rule-consequentialism is indeed a lost cause if one accepts an overarching commitment to maximize the good. This need not be the death knell of rule-consequentialism. For the best argument for rule-consequentialism is *not* that it derives from an overarching commitment to maximize the good. The best argument for rule-consequentialism is that it does a better job than its rivals of matching and tying together our moral convictions, as well as offering us help with our moral disagreements and uncertainties.

This might also address a related worry: that rule consequentialism collapses into act consequentialism. If following the rules maximizes the good, then it is as if we should just follow one rule: maximize the good. But, on one interpretation at least, Hooker does not advocate for a set of rules picked solely on the basis that they maximize the good.

Another difficulty, however, stems from the fact that rule consequentialism has to take into account the costs of inculcating the rules. According to Ross, we have fundamental duties of fidelity and gratitude towards our friends. The rule consequentialist, on the other hand, has to ask what impact incorporating rules concerning loyalty and gratitude would have on expected value. Suppose that a world in which we treat everyone impartially would be better than one in which we display partiality, leaving considerations of cost aside. I don't endorse this view; but the point is that the rule consequentialist has to include such costs in their calculations – and Hooker concludes that they 'outweigh the benefits' of an impartial world:

> Imagine what psychological and financial resources would have to be devoted to getting the overwhelming majority of children in each new generation to internalize an overriding equal concern for all others! The costs would outweigh the benefits. (Hooker, 2000: 141)

These cost considerations are completely alien to the deontological perspective. Fidelity, for instance, is basic. It is not something that has to be justified by appeal to something more fundamental – and certainly not on the grounds that it's too expensive to stamp out.

And rule consequentialism's requirement that inculcation costs be considered leads to further implausible consequences. Imagine, for example, a world in which people take great pleasure in torturing cats, and in which it would be so expensive to get the population to internalize a rule prohibiting this practice that the costs would outweigh the benefits. Thus, according to rule consequentialism, torturing cats for fun would be morally permissible in such a world. This, of course, the deontologist adamantly denies.

It might be claimed, however, that Rossian deontology is objectionably conservative in a way that rule consequentialism is not. The Rossian deontologist relies upon careful and critical reflection in determining both what the prima facie duties are, and how they apply in a given circumstance, and this reflection is inevitably shaped by her moral education and cultural milieu. Thus, the objection runs, the morality she advocates will likely comport with the traditions of her society. Rule consequentialism, on the other hand, in looking to the good to help determine the rules, can depart more radically from traditional mores. Or so it might be argued.

First, however, it is hard to see how, in arriving at an account of the good, the rule consequentialist is not going to have to critically reflect on what is valuable (see Hooker, 2000: 106), so that the same difficulty arises as for the Rossian: the rule consequentialist's account of what is good, and hence the rules she proposes, are both going to be influenced by her moral education and cultural milieu.

Second, as we saw, Hooker (2000: 101), in defending rule consequentialism, appeals to the claim that 'it does a better job than its rivals of matching and tying together our moral convictions'. But presumably these moral convictions are considered moral judgements, which we arrive at via reflection, just as does the Rossian, so that, as Hooker notes (2000: 107), rule consequentialism and Rossian deontology largely agree in their prescriptions, hence neither is more conservative than the other. Furthermore, moral reflection is critical, so that considered moral judgement can depart markedly from tradition.

We could only, of course, have an external check on our moral reflections if we had another way of getting at the truth. And the Kantian might be seen as attempting to do this by generating morality from a fundamental principle of rationality (the categorical imperative). In the next section, I revisit this idea, but even the Kantian enterprise is not free from appeal to moral reflection: when an output of the categorical imperative clashes with considered moral judgement, the response on the part of the Kantian is likely to be, not that the judgement is incorrect, but that the categorical imperative has been misapplied. Considered moral judgements are the standard against which moral theories are tested.

5 Normativity, Motivation, and Practical Reasons

Practical reasons, and the contrasts between Ross and Kant, have been discussed in Sections 1.2 and 1.5, respectively, but in this section I briefly discuss some more foundational issues.

Ross was an advocate of intuitionism, which is a form of (practical) normative realism, according to which, in addition to non-normative facts, such as the fact that it is cold, there are normative facts, such as the fact that it is cold is a reason for you to wear your coat. Normative facts are facts about what we ought to, or have reason to, believe or do. Theoretical deliberation concerns what we have reason to believe. Practical deliberation concerns what we have reason (including moral reason) to do. On Ross's view (as I am interpreting it), facts about what we have a duty to do are normative facts to the effect that we have moral reasons to do such things as keep our promises. And a further component of the view is that these normative facts are metaphysically basic: they are not dependent on something more fundamental. One upshot is that the question, 'Why be moral?', if asked in search of non-moral reasons to behave as morality requires (and do things such as generally keep your promises), is shut off: there are fundamental moral reasons.

However, reasons motivate people to do things, so how can facts accomplish this? *Externalists* about motivation see it as possible that someone might believe she has a reason to do some act, and yet not be motivated in the least to do it.

Internalists deny this. Intuitionism is consistent with either view. Suppose I believe that Eve has a headache and an aspirin will relieve it. And suppose I also believe that the fact just cited is a reason for me to give Eve an aspirin. On the externalist view, I will be motivated to give Eve an aspirin just in case I have a desire (which I might lack) to do what I take myself to have reason to do. But on the internalist account my belief that I have (moral) reason to give Eve an aspirin brings with it a motivation to do so. On either account there are two beliefs here: my belief that Eve has a headache and an aspirin will relieve it, and my belief that this is a reason to give her one. If things are going well, first, I have the beliefs in question because it is true both that Eve has a headache and that this is a reason for me to give her an aspirin; and, second, these beliefs of mine motivate me to give Eve an aspirin. Internalism simply limits the possibilities for motivational malfunction: I cannot fail to be motivated to give Eve an aspirin if I believe I have reason to do so.

For the intuitionist, then, reasons, and the fact that they are reasons, explain agents' beliefs that they have reasons to do things; and these beliefs play a crucial role in agents' motivations. When an agent sees the world aright, she is motivated to act in some way because she has reason to. But on certain Kantian constructivist (see Section 1.5) accounts, by contrast, a rational agent has a reason to do some act only when, and because, she is motivated to do it: the direction of explanation is reversed.

For example, according to Darwall (in Copp, 2006: 299):

> In [the Kantians'] view ... something's standing as a normative reason ultimately depends on its being motivating (treated as a reason) in fully rational deliberation, where the latter is determined by internal, formal features of the deliberative process, not by its responsiveness to independently establishable normative reasons.

So, according to Darwall's Kantian, that, say, an utterance would be a lie is a reason not to utter it because any fully rational agent is motivated not to lie, where to be fully rational, in part at least, is to act only on principles that pass the categorical imperative test.

The intuitionist, on the other hand, claims that there *are* 'independently establishable normative reasons'. Suppose that if A were to utter S she would be lying; and suppose further that this is a reason for A not to utter S. If A is virtuous (or fully rational, in Kantian terms) and grasps these facts, she will be motivated not to utter S. But she will be so motivated because she has reason not to utter S and sees this – on the intuitionist account the fact that an idealized agent is motivated not to utter S does nothing to make it the case that there is a reason not to utter it.

The Rossian intuitionist takes there to be normative facts – about what our prima facie duties are, about whether an act falls under any of them (hence about what you have moral reason to do), and about what we are morally required to do. We arrive at knowledge of these facts through reflection upon, and wise judgement about, cases, both actual and possible. From the Kantian perspective, however, these judgements comprise unsubstantiated moral assumptions. The application of the categorical imperative, on the other hand, requires no substantive – that is, moral or evaluational – input: it is a formal rather than a substantive procedure (or so it is claimed). And while moral judgement at some points is required on the Kantian approach – for example, it is a Kantian requirement that we help strangers, and judgement is required to determine how and when to do this – applying the categorical imperative does not require the making of moral judgements. On the intuitionist approach, by contrast, moral judgement is required at all points. There is no procedure, let alone a formal procedure, for determining what our prima facie duties are, which of them an act falls under, or how to weigh their relative importance in cases of conflict.

The intuitionist, in addition to seeing the Kantian procedure as putting the cart before the horse when it comes to the direction of both moral and motivational explanation, also sees the Kantian procedure as often questionable in its application and incorrect in its verdicts. And even when the verdict is correct, the procedure is in danger of failing to furnish the correct reason for action (see Section 1.5). Finally, the intuitionist claims that any principles generated by a Kantian procedure must conform to our antecedent reflective judgements, so that the procedure is at best redundant.

Nevertheless, many critics see intuitionism as insufficiently 'principled', and, from this perspective, at least Kantians are proposing a decision procedure. And even if Kantianism fails in its current form, perhaps with sufficient ingenuity it can be saved (see, e.g., Parfit, 2011, Parts 2 and 3).

From the Kantian side, then, intuitionism, and Ross in particular, are attacked for their over-reliance on judgement, and lack of formal procedures. However, the Rossian intuitionist does subscribe to some principles – the prima facie duties. I turn now to an attack from the other direction: some see Rossian intuitionism as *too* principled.

6 The Place of Moral Principles

6.1 Generalism or Particularism?

What is the role of moral principles in ethics? There is a spectrum of views: at one end there are those generalists who hold that the job of moral philosophy is to refine our principles so that they can be used with precision to deliver clear verdicts.

This is to understand morality by analogy with law (as the common phrase 'the moral law' implies). Written laws try to define as precisely as possible exactly what actions constitute a legal offence. And where statutes fail in this regard, judicial decisions make laws more precise and set a precedent that guides later judgements.

At the other end, extreme particularists[11] (as they are known – the coinage is Hare's, 1963: 18) have denied the very existence of useful moral principles. Each particular case is different, and appeal to principles, it is feared, oversimplifies and distorts the nature of moral thinking, downplaying the role of imagination and judgement in the morally sensitive person's assessment of what should be done in *this* case. This is to understand morality by analogy with aesthetic judgement. Attempts to lay down rules of aesthetic appreciation appear ridiculous; each work of art has to be judged on its own individual merits.

Where is Ross on this spectrum? While he is not a particularist, since principles play a role, that role is significantly limited, in a number of ways. First, as we have seen, Ross holds that appeal to principles cannot settle what to do in conflict cases, and for Ross conflict is the norm, since there is nearly always something to be said on both sides. Ross offers very little general guidance for resolving conflicts; he offers a few remarks about the comparative stringency of the prima facie duties – that fidelity is usually a more weighty duty than beneficence, for example – but that is all. For the rest, Ross says, citing Aristotle, the decision rests with perception, that is, sensitivity to the details of the particular case.

> This sense of our particular duty in particular circumstances, preceded and informed by the fullest reflection we can bestow on the act in all its bearings, is highly fallible, but it is the only guide we have to our duty. (1930: 42)

Even deciding whether an act falls under one of Ross's prima facie duties often requires judgement. Take non-maleficence. Philosophers have spilled much ink trying to provide a watertight account of when someone has violated a duty not to harm. Ross seems to have little interest in attempting to make the harm principle more precise. That may be because the notion of harm itself eludes codification.

Furthermore, Ross's methodology, as we have seen, is 'bottom-up' rather than 'top-down'. A top-down theory, such as Kant's, holds that we start by appeal to plausible abstract principles which we then use to determine what is morally relevant, and which types of act are required, permissible, or forbidden.

---

[11] See Dancy (2017) and Ridge and McKeever (2020) for further details and references.

For Ross, justification goes in the reverse direction. We frame our principles in the light of what we judge about particular cases. Indeed, Ross holds that basic principles play no role in helping us derive the moral character of an act. He asks, 'Once the general principles have been reached, are particular acts recognized as right by deduction from general principles, or by direct reflection on the acts as particular acts having a certain character?' (1939: 171). He claims that the latter is virtually always the case. But if I can tell straight off, without appeal to principles, that, say, its cruelty would count against this action, the principles do no epistemic work. (See also Section 3.5.)

Particularism began as a challenge to the claim that there are moral principles of the kind Ross proposes. Certainly, some of Ross's own principles (as laid out in Ross, 1930; but see also Ross, 1939) seem vulnerable to counterexamples. Does a promise to do a wicked deed give me *some* reason, however weak, to do it? If my benefactor helped me by perpetrating some horrendous crime, do I have any reason to be grateful? In just punishment, does not the fact that it will harm the guilty person count as a reason in favour of inflicting the penalty, rather than against? Those who think that there must be general moral principles will respond by insisting that the principle needs more careful formulation to make it immune to counterexample: there is moral reason not to harm the *innocent*; promises are only binding under certain conditions (see Ross, 1939, chapter 5), and so on. There is a danger of a dialectical stand-off here. The particularist will try to provide ingenious counterexamples to the qualified principles; the principlist will seek to add yet more riders and qualifications to deal with those counterexamples. This process can go on indefinitely without a decisive victory by either side.

Attention has increasingly turned, however, to the question of whether there *must* be moral principles,[12] even if it is difficult to formulate them precisely. We have seen that Ross denies that principles are epistemically required, but he may think of them as an ineliminable feature of the moral landscape nonetheless. According to the particularist, whether or not you think there must be principles depends on whether you have a holistic or an atomistic conception of reasons. The holist contends that a consideration that counts in favour of an action in one

---

[12] Care must be taken here not to fall prey to a standard logical fallacy. For example, a good state of the world is made good by its further features (and the degrees to which they are present). So there may be a tendency to conclude from this that there is a list of invariantly good-making features that make all good states good. Similarly, the moral status of an act depends upon its non-moral features, so perhaps we might conclude that there is a list of, say, invariantly wrong-making features that, when present to the right degrees, make all wrong acts wrong. But neither conclusion follows by logic alone. (Otherwise we could conclude from the fact that everyone has a mother that there is some poor woman who is the mother of everyone.) If the general claim is made, then, that there simply must be moral principles, or invariant reasons, this needs substantive argument.

circumstance can be irrelevant to it, or even count against it, in another. Every act has a unique context, and, says the holist, the reason-giving force of any given consideration is dependent upon other considerations present in the case, where this dependence defies codification. To employ a chemical analogy, the valence of any consideration can switch from case to case.[13] So, for example, that an act will give pleasure has positive valence when the pleasure is innocent, but negative valence when the pleasure is sadistic. It is generally accepted that many reasons change valence in this way, but the atomist holds that at the level of fundamental considerations valence must be unchanging. And this may be Ross's view.

In Section 3.1, I attributed to Ross the view that fundamental considerations are morally significant in their own right and thus always carry moral weight. That an act would violate fidelity, for instance, is a bedrock proposition in that there is no more fundamental duty from which that of fidelity arises – and this entails, on the view I am attributing to Ross, that violating fidelity has invariantly negative valence (that an act would violate fidelity always counts against it). But does this entailment hold? I think not. That we have arrived at bedrock when we see that some act would violate fidelity does not entail that fidelity violation *always* counts against an act. The fact that we cannot, as it were, dig any deeper does not entail that the adjacent terrain makes no difference. Perhaps an analogy from epistemology might help. You declare that this shirt is red on the basis that it appears so to you. And there is nothing more fundamental to be said. But this doesn't entail that seeming red always indicates redness. While nothing more fundamental can be said than that the shirt appears red, there are plenty of 'surrounding features' that are relevant – such as the fact that you are not wearing colour-distorting spectacles. Ross, on this portrayal, is tacitly assuming that, because a consideration is fundamental, its reason-giving force is thus completely independent of any other facts of the case in question. But this assumption is subject to challenge.

I agree with Dancy (2004: 119) that we have yet to see a good argument in favour of the claim that there must be invariant reasons. But this does not close off the possibility that there are some.

It is useful at this point to single out principles whose content can only be couched in normative terms. (Usage varies, but I am using the term 'normative' to include the evaluative.) The principle, 'Don't inflict pain', is not normative in

---

[13] Note that switching valence is simply an extreme case of changing strength, and it is a commonplace that reasons change strength from case to case. The diminishing marginal utility of money is an obvious example: the strength of your reason to earn an extra dollar depends on how much money you have at the time.

this sense: whether an act inflicts pain is not a normative matter. The duty of non-maleficence, on the other hand, employs the notion of harm, which is ineliminably normative: to harm someone is not merely to inflict pain on them, it is to make them *worse* off. (There is, of course, a lively and long-term debate about whether the normative can be reduced in some way to the non-normative. As is apparent from this paragraph, I deny that it can be.)

One form of particularism claims that no *non-normative* features have invariant valence. This seems plausible. Take pain again. At first thought, the fact that an act would cause someone pain might be taken always to count against it. But what about masochists? So then we might try: the fact that an act would cause someone to endure something she dislikes always counts against it. But what about the case of justified punishment? The fact that the felon dislikes imprisonment is part of the reason *for* imprisoning him.

But even if non-normative features lack invariant valence, the contextual variance might be limited, so that any exceptions could be incorporated into moral principles (painful sensations count against unless. . .). But the holism that particularism espouses is more radical than that – it claims that for any finite principle we come up with, we cannot know in advance whether there might not be an unforeseen context in which it fails to deliver the correct verdict.

While I am sympathetic to this claim – that there are no *non-normative* features that have invariant valence – there may nevertheless be *normative* features that do. So, for example, that an act would be unjust is, it would seem, always a reason against doing it. And while the fact that the act would be harmful may not always count against it, the fact that it would harm an innocent seems to.[14]

As far as moral reasoning goes, perhaps morality might have been completely unprincipled – principles may not be epistemically necessary. Indeed, as already noted, Ross himself insists that we are capable of picking out what is morally relevant in the particular case without appeal to general principles, thus he has no need to claim that such principles *must* be available for this purpose. Nevertheless, it is noteworthy that the prima facie duties have normative content, which is why moral sensitivity is required to apply them correctly, and, even if they are not quite correct in their details, the idea that there are normative features with invariant valence could nonetheless be right.

---

[14] Here is a potential counterexample. A mobster threatens that unless you harm an innocent or do something unjust he's going to do something far worse. Thus the fact that your act will harm an innocent or be unjust appears to count in its favour here. But there are various responses. For example, it's the fact that your act would appease the mobster that counts in its favour; the fact that it would be unjust or harm an innocent counts against it. The mobster is trying to get you to do something that you have reason not to do by providing a stronger reason for you to do it.

But if it is wrong, as the radical particularist suggests, then it might seem that morality lacks structure. However, the particularist denies that the only way a moral outlook can be coherent and structured is by resting on a few general moral principles. The notion that the judgements someone makes in different cases can cohere only if they are underpinned by general principles is, she claims, a generalist prejudice.

6.2 Virtue Ethics

Another approach that eschews exceptionless moral principles is virtue ethics (see Hursthouse and Pettigrove, 2018). The virtue theorist sees the virtues (such as compassion, courage, fidelity, generosity, honesty, and kindness) as not only valuable in their own right, but also instrumentally so: the virtuous can discern what is morally salient in any particular situation, and reliably choose the right act. But they do not do this by applying an algorithm. Rather, like Ross and the particularist, the virtue ethicist insists that there is no algorithmic decision procedure for working out the right thing to do; rather, this requires good moral judgement, which involves the sensitivity, experience, and discernment possessed by the virtuous. Furthermore, the virtues play a crucial role in motivation: the virtuous agent not only does the right thing, but does it for the right motives. Thus moral philosophy should focus, says the virtue theorist, more on what kind of person to be, rather than on trying to find exceptionless moral principles.

However, there are (at least) two views concerning the purport of virtue ethics. On the less radical, the virtues are seen as coequal with other practical normative notions: the former are not grounded in the latter and vice versa. And virtue ethics is proposed as a corrective to views that focus on attempting to formulate moral decision procedures. On the more radical view, by contrast, virtue ethics is put forward as a complete alternative theory in its own right, with virtues and vices, and the corresponding judgements of the virtuous, being foundational, and grounding the other normative concepts.

The less radical approach comports with the broadly Rossian deontology I favour, which agrees that overly principled approaches distort moral thinking by downplaying the need for judgement and imagination in discerning which features of a case are relevant, how they interact with each other, and what weight should be given to each. But I am sceptical of the more radical approach, which maintains that the right is metaphysically dependent upon the judgements of the virtuous. In difficult cases we may have no *epistemic* access to which act is right other than via the judgement of virtuous agents. But the virtuous agent judges an act right because it is right, not the other way around. Otherwise, on what does she base her judgement? It must be responsive to her reasons, and those reasons, if she is appropriately sensitive, lead her to the correct verdict about what she should do. Thus, assuming the reasons are those endorsed by the deontologist, virtue ethics might best be seen as a component of deontology.

This opinion is reinforced by one response to the charge that virtue ethics is insufficiently action-guiding. Virtue ethics, Hursthouse (1999) suggests, following Anscombe, could provide guidance by incorporating rules employing the virtue and vice terms – rules such as 'do what is charitable, and avoid doing what is uncharitable'. But, on one reading,[15] this is just another way of stating Ross's prima facie duty of beneficence. And the same might apply to other such rules, mutatis mutandis.

---

[15] On a different reading, two differences may be that doing what is charitable requires acting from a particular motive, whereas Ross denies that it is ever our duty to act from a motive (1930: 4–6), and, relatedly, doing what is charitable may not succeed in actually being beneficent – despite intentions, a charitable act may fail to better the condition of others.

References

Alexander, L. and Moore, M. (2016) 'Deontological Ethics'. *The Stanford Encyclopedia of Philosophy* (Winter 2016 ed.), Edward N. Zalta (ed.), https://plato.stanford.edu/archives/win2016/entries/ethics-deontological/.

Aquinas, T. (1988) (13th c). '*Summa Theologica II-II*, Q. 64, art. 7, "Of Killing"'. In Baumgarth, W. P. and Regan, R. J. (eds.) *On Law, Morality, and Politics*, Indianapolis, IN: Hackett, 226–7.

Audi, R. (1996) 'Intuitionism, Pluralism, and the Foundations of Ethics'. In Sinnott-Armstrong, W. and Timmons, M. (eds.) *Moral Knowledge: New Readings in Moral Epistemology*, Oxford: Oxford University Press, 101–36.

Audi, R. (2004) *The Good in the Right: A Theory of Intuition and Intrinsic Value*, Princeton, NJ: Princeton University Press.

Broad, C. D. (1930) *Five Types of Ethical Theory*, New York: Harcourt, Brace.

Copp, D. (ed.) (2006) *Oxford Handbook of Ethical Theory*, Oxford: Oxford University Press.

Dancy, J. (1998) 'Wiggins and Ross'. *Utilitas*, 10: 281–5.

Dancy, J. (2004) *Ethics without Principles*, Oxford: Clarendon Press.

Dancy, J. (2017) 'Moral Particularism'. *The Stanford Encyclopedia of Philosophy* (Winter 2017 ed.), Edward N. Zalta (ed.), https://plato.stanford.edu/archives/win2017/entries/moral-particularism/.

Daniels, N. (2020) 'Reflective Equilibrium'. *The Stanford Encyclopedia of Philosophy* (Summer 2020 ed.), Edward N. Zalta (ed.), https://plato.stanford.edu/archives/sum2020/entries/reflective-equilibrium/.

Darwall, S. (1998) 'Under Moore's Spell'. *Utilitas*, 10: 286–91.

Darwall, S. (2006) 'Morality and Practical Reason: A Kantian Approach' in Copp 2006, 282–320.

Dreier, J. (2011) 'In Defense of Consequentializing'. In Timmons, M. (ed.) *Oxford Studies in Normative Ethics*, Volume 1, Oxford: Oxford University Press, 97–119.

Ebels-Duggan, K. (2011) 'Kantian Ethics'. In Miller, C. (ed.) *The Continuum Companion to Ethics*, London: Bloomsbury, 168–89.

FitzPatrick, W. J. (2012) 'The Doctrine of Double Effect: Intention and Permissibility'. *Philosophy Compass*, 7(3): 183–96.

Fohr, S. A. (1998) 'The Double Effect of Pain Medication: Separating Myth from Reality'. *Journal of Palliative Medicine*, 1: 315–28.

Foot, P. (1967) 'The Problem of Abortion and the Doctrine of Double Effect'. *Oxford Review* No. 5 (reprinted in *Virtues and Vices and Other Essays*, Berkeley, CA: University of California Press, 1978).

Geach, P. T. (1956) 'Good and Evil'. *Analysis*, 17: 32–42.

Hare, R. (1963) *Freedom and Reason*, Oxford: Oxford University Press.

Hooker, B. (2000) *Ideal Code, Real World*, Oxford: Clarendon Press.

Hursthouse, R. (1999) *On Virtue Ethics*, Oxford: Oxford University Press.

Hursthouse, R. and Pettigrove, G. (2018) 'Virtue Ethics'. *The Stanford Encyclopedia of Philosophy* (Winter 2018 ed.), Edward N. Zalta (ed.), https://plato.stanford.edu/archives/win2018/entries/ethics-virtue/.

Jackson, M. and Smith, M. (2006) 'Absolutist Moral Theories and Uncertainty'. *The Journal of Philosophy*, 103(6): 267–83.

Jamieson, D. (ed.) (1999) *Singer and His Critics*, Hoboken, NJ: Wiley.

Johnson, R. and Cureton, A. (2021) 'Kant's Moral Philosophy'. *The Stanford Encyclopedia of Philosophy* (Spring 2021 ed.), Edward N. Zalta (ed.), https://plato.stanford.edu/archives/spr2021/entries/kant-moral/.

Kagan, S. (1984) 'Does Consequentialism Demand Too Much?' *Philosophy and Public Affairs*, 13: 239–54.

Kagan, S. (1989) *The Limits of Morality*, Oxford: Clarendon Press.

Kant, I. (1993) [1785] *Grounding for the Metaphysics of Morals*, 3rd ed., translated by J. W. Ellington, Indianapolis, IN: Hackett.

Kant, I. (2015) [1788] *Critique of Practical Reason*, rev. ed., translated by M. Gregor, translation revised by A. Reath, Cambridge: Cambridge University Press.

Katz, L. (1996) *Ill-Gotten Gains: Evasion, Blackmail, Fraud and Kindred Puzzles of the Law*, Chicago, IL: University of Chicago Press.

Kavka, G. S. (1983) 'The Toxin Puzzle'. *Analysis*, 43(1): 33–6.

Mackie, J. (1977) *Ethics: Inventing Right and Wrong*, Harmondsworth: Penguin Books.

McIntyre, A. (2019) 'Doctrine of Double Effect'. *The Stanford Encyclopedia of Philosophy* (Spring 2019 ed.), Edward N. Zalta (ed.), https://plato.stanford.edu/archives/spr2019/entries/double-effect/.

McNaughton, D. and Rawling, P. (1991) 'Agent-Relativity and the Doing–Happening Distinction'. *Philosophical Studies*, 63: 167–85.

McNaughton, D. and Rawling, P. (2006) 'Deontology'. In Copp 2006, 424–58.

McNaughton, D. and Rawling, P. (2013) 'Intuitionism'. In LaFollette, H. and Persson, I. (eds.) *The Blackwell Guide to Ethical Theory*, 2nd ed., Hoboken, NJ: Wiley-Blackwell, 287–310.

Moore, G. E. (1966) [1903] *Principia Ethica*, Cambridge: Cambridge University Press.

Moore, G. E. (1912) *Ethics*, London: Williams & Norgate.

Moran, K. A. (2022) *Kant's Ethics*, Cambridge: Cambridge University Press

Nagel, T. (1970) *The Possibility of Altruism*, Princeton, NJ: Princeton University Press.

Nagel, T. (1986) *The View from Nowhere*, Oxford: Oxford University Press.

Nelkin, D. K. and Rickless, S. C. (2014) 'Three Cheers for Double Effect'. *Philosophy and Phenomenological Research*, 89(1): 125–58.

Parfit, D. (1984) *Reason and Persons*, Oxford: Oxford University Press.

Parfit, D. (2011) *On What Matters*, Oxford: Oxford University Press.

Pettit, P. (1987) 'Universalizability without Utilitarianism'. *Mind*, 96: 74–82.

Phillips, D. (2019) *Rossian Ethics: W.D. Ross and Contemporary Moral Theory*, Oxford: Oxford University Press.

Portmore, D. (2011) *Commonsense Consequentialism: Wherein Morality Meets Rationality*, Oxford: Oxford University Press.

Portmore, D. (ed.) (2020) *The Oxford Handbook of Consequentialism*, Oxford: Oxford University Press.

Quinn, W. S. (1989a) 'Actions, Intentions, and Consequences: The Doctrine of Double Effect'. *Philosophy and Public Affairs*, 18: 334–51.

Quinn, W. S. (1989b) 'Actions, Intentions, and Consequences: The Doctrine of Doing and Allowing'. *Philosophical Review*, 98(3): 287–312.

Rachels, J. (1975) 'Active and Passive Euthanasia'. *New England Journal of Medicine*, 292: 78–86.

Ridge, M. and McKeever, S. (2020) 'Moral Particularism and Moral Generalism'. *The Stanford Encyclopedia of Philosophy* (Winter 2020 ed.), Edward N. Zalta (ed.), https://plato.stanford.edu/archives/win2020/entries/moral-particularism-generalism/.

Rohlf, M. (2020) 'Immanuel Kant'. *The Stanford Encyclopedia of Philosophy* (Fall 2020 ed.), Edward N. Zalta (ed.), https://plato.stanford.edu/archives/fall2020/entries/kant/.

Ross, W. D. (1930) *The Right and the Good*, Indianapolis, IN: Hackett.

Ross, W. D. (1939) *The Foundations of Ethics*, Oxford: Clarendon Press.

Scanlon, T. M. (1998) *What We Owe to Each Other*, Cambridge, MA: Harvard University Press.

Scanlon, T. M. (2008) *Moral Dimensions: Permissibility, Meaning, Blame*, Cambridge, MA: Belknap Press of Harvard University Press.

Scheffler, S. (ed.) (1988) *Consequentialism and Its Critics*, Oxford: Oxford University Press.

Scheffler, S. (1994) *The Rejection of Consequentialism*, rev. ed., Oxford: Clarendon Press.

Singer, P. (1972) 'Famine, Affluence, and Morality'. *Philosophy & Public Affairs*, 1(3): 229–43.

Snow, N. E. (2020) *Contemporary Virtue Ethics*, Cambridge: Cambridge University Press.

Suikkanen, J. (2020) *Contractualism*, Cambridge: Cambridge University Press.

Sykes, N. and Thorns, A. (2003) 'The Use of Opioids and Sedatives at the End of Life'. *The Lancet Oncology*, 1: 312–18.

Taurek, J. M. (1977) 'Should the Numbers Count?' *Philosophy and Public Affairs*, 6(4): 293–316.

Thomson, J. J. (1985) 'The Trolley Problem'. *The Yale Law Journal*, 94(6): 1395–415.

Thomson, J. J. (2008) 'Turning the Trolley'. *Philosophy and Public Affairs*, 36(4): 359–74.

Wiggins, D. (1998) '*The Right and the Good* and W. D. Ross's Criticism of Consequentialism'. *Utilitas*, 10: 261–80.

Woollard, F. (2012a) 'The Doctrine of Doing and Allowing I: Analysis of the Doing/Allowing Distinction'. *Philosophy Compass*, 7(7): 448–58.

Woollard, F. (2012b) 'The Doctrine of Doing and Allowing II: The Moral Relevance of the Doing/Allowing Distinction'. *Philosophy Compass*, 7(7) 459–69.

Woollard, F. and Howard-Snyder, F. (2021) 'Doing vs. Allowing Harm'. *The Stanford Encyclopedia of Philosophy* (Fall 2021 ed.), Edward N. Zalta (ed.), https://plato.stanford.edu/archives/fall2021/entries/doing-allowing/.

Acknowledgements

This Element owes much to my frequent collaborator, David McNaughton, who first introduced me to theorizing about ethics over thirty years ago, and has been my guide ever since. Indeed, the Element draws on previous work of ours: see, for example, McNaughton and Rawling, 1991, 2006, 2013. I would also like to thank two anonymous referees, and two very tolerant editors, Dale Miller and Ben Eggleston. This Element is introductory in nature, as befits an Element, so I have set aside many complications and qualifications.

Cambridge Elements $^{\equiv}$

Ethics

Ben Eggleston

University of Kansas

Ben Eggleston is a professor of philosophy at the University of Kansas. He is the editor of John Stuart Mill, *Utilitarianism: With Related Remarks from Mill's Other Writings* (Hackett, 2017) and a co-editor of *Moral Theory and Climate Change: Ethical Perspectives on a Warming Planet* (Routledge, 2020), *The Cambridge Companion to Utilitarianism* (Cambridge, 2014), and *John Stuart Mill and the Art of Life* (Oxford, 2011). He is also the author of numerous articles and book chapters on various topics in ethics.

Dale E. Miller

Old Dominion University, Virginia

Dale E. Miller is a professor of philosophy at Old Dominion University. He is the author of *John Stuart Mill: Moral, Social and Political Thought* (Polity, 2010) and a co-editor of *Moral Theory and Climate Change: Ethical Perspectives on a Warming Planet* (Routledge, 2020), *A Companion to Mill* (Blackwell, 2017), *The Cambridge Companion to Utilitarianism* (Cambridge, 2014), *John Stuart Mill and the Art of Life* (Oxford, 2011), and *Morality, Rules, and Consequences: A Critical Reader* (Edinburgh, 2000). He is also the editor-in-chief of *Utilitas*, and the author of numerous articles and book chapters on various topics in ethics broadly construed.

About the Series

This Elements series provides an extensive overview of major figures, theories, and concepts in the field of ethics. Each entry in the series acquaints students with the main aspects of its topic while articulating the author's distinctive viewpoint in a manner that will interest researchers.

Cambridge Elements ☰

Ethics

Printed in the United States
by Baker & Taylor Publisher Services